THE PIP ANTHOLOGY OF WORLD POETRY
OF THE 20TH CENTURY
VOLUME 2

GREEN INTEGER
6026 Wilshire Boulevard
Los Angeles, California 90036

(323) 857-1115 FAX: (323) 857-0143
E-Mail: djmess@greeninteger.com
visit our web-site: www.greeninteger.com

Douglas Messerli, Publisher

THE PIP

ANTHOLOGY OF WORLD POETRY
OF THE 20TH CENTURY

VOLUME 2

*Edited with a Note
by Douglas Messerli*

EL-E-PHANT 2

GREEN INTEGER
KØBENHAVN & LOS ANGELES
2001

GREEN INTEGER BOOKS
Edited by Per Bregne
København/Los Angeles

Distributed in the United States by Consortium Book
Sales and Distribution, 1045 Westgate Drive, Suite 90
Saint Paul, Minnesota 55114-1065

(323) 857-1115/http://www.greeninteger.com

First edition published 2001
Copyright ©2001 by Douglas Messerli
All permissions for the publication of poetry appear
at the end of each poet's section of this book.
Back cover copy ©2001 by Green Integer

Design: Douglas Messerli
Photographs and drawings: left to right, top to bottom
Anna Akhmatova (drawing by Amedeo Modigliani); Gottfried Benn (photo by Ullstein);
Blaise Cendrars (drawing by Francis Picabia); Saint-John Perse; Edith Södergran;
Oswald de Andrade; Barbara Guest (photo by Star Black);
Forugh Farrokhazad (self-portrait); Maruyama Kaoru.
Typography: Guy Bennett

LIBRARY OF CONGRESS CATALOGING IN PUBLICATION DATA
Messerli, Douglas, ed. [1947]
The PIP Anthology of World Poetry
of the 20th Century
Volume 2
ISBN: 1-892295-94-6
p. cm — Green Integer / EL-E-PHANT 2
I. Title II. Series III.

Green Integer books are published for Douglas Messerli
Printed in the United States of America on acid-free paper.

TABLE OF CONTENTS

A NOTE

The success of the first volume of the *PIP Anthology of World Poetry in the 20th Century*, published in 2000, has encouraged me to continue on the road of an ongoing series of anthologies, ultimately including the work of more than 500 twentieth century poets.

As I noted in the first volume, I believe it necessary to understand modern poetry in the context of the international in order to comprehend the genius of the poetry of the past century. Unfortunately, many cultures—certainly it can be said of the American poetry scene—tend to focus, at times, on their own precedents, and accordingly, often miss the creative stimulation that is available to them in good translations. There is no question that my writing has only been enhanced by all the international reading I have done in the past few years. Certainly, it has allowed me to expand my own limitations and to understand writing in a much larger context. Several of my knowledgable poet friends, moreover, discovered new poetic figures in the first volume—exactly what I had hoped for. I believe the subsequent volumes will continue that excitement.

As we began collecting the writing, it has also become apparent that there needed to be a tool that could provide readers with information about new works, translations and other pertinent material about the poets as we proceed. So in this second volume, I have added a section titled *News and Additions*, which I will continue and expand in each subsequent volume. As promised, the index includes the names of all poets published to date with the volume and page numbers. Moreover, the poems included in the second volume are also listed in this index.

Once again I must thank dear friends and supporters who have helped to accomplish the near-impossible tasks which I have laid out for myself: Charles Bernstein, Jerome Rothenberg, Christopher Middleton, Michael Henry Heim, Pierre Joris, Rick Gilbert, Michael Hamburger, Hiroaki Sato, Marjorie Perloff, and Murat Nemat-Nejat have offered important suggestions and research for this and future volumes. The Young Research Library of the University of California, Los Angeles has continued to be the center of my research, and its staff and faculty have helped me in innumerable ways. Guy Bennett has continued to be central to this volume in his work with translation and with typography; Diana Daves cheerfully reads the voluminous material I send her way with great skill and acumen; Kate Wolf and other interns have continued to provide invaluable help in the preparation of each volume. And all the translators and publishers mentioned within have made this volume possible.

—DOUGLAS MESSERLI

Anna Akhmatova [Russia]
1889–1966

Born Anna Andreevna Gorenko on June 23, 1889, Akhmatova grew up in Tsarskoye Selo near St. Petersburg, Russia. In 1903 she met the young Russian poet Nikolai Gumilev, whose desperate courtship of her served as the subject of many of the poems she began writing in 1905. In 1910 Gumilev and Akhmatova were married near Kiev. After their honeymoon in Paris, they settled in Tsarskoye Selo, with Gumilev returning to Abyssinia on a scientific expedition later that year. In 1911 Gumilev returned, and the couple again traveled to Paris where Akhmatova met the artist Amedeo Modigliani. Upon their return to Russia they involved themselves in an active literary life, forming a Poets' Guild, whose members broke with the dominant Symbolism of

Drawing by Amedeo Modigliani

the time. Six poets—Gumilev, Akhmatova, Osip Mandelshtam [see *The PIP Anthology, Vol. 1*, pp. 125–132], Sergei Gorodetski, Vladimir Narbut and Mikhail Zenkevich—joined forces, calling themselves the Acmeists. Their poetry focused upon a vivid representation and direct statement of life. In 1912 Akhmatova's first book of poetry, *Evening*, was published, followed by *Rosary* (1914), both of which were immediately successful in pre-revolutionary Russia.

A son, Lev, was born to the Gumilevs in 1912, but over the next few years Akhmatova would be able to spend little time with her husband. In the spring of 1913 he returned to Abyssinia as director of an expedition by the Academy of Sciences, and the following year he volunteered for the Russian front of World War I. 1915 began the long decline of health and well-being for Akhmatova. Her father died in Petersburg and, in the autumn, she was diagnosed with tuberculosis. In 1917, the year of the revolution, Akhmatova and Gumilev separated and divorced the following year. That same year she published *White Flock*, dedicating the poems to her artist-friend Boris Anrep, who soon after left Russia, never to return. As Lenin and the Bolshviks seized power, Akhmatova married Vladimir Shileiko, like Gumilev an Assyriologist by profession. That winter was one of great privation and cold. The following year saw the instigation of the Red Terror against opponents of the new Soviet regime. Gumilev was shot by a firing squad in 1921. In the same year, Akhmatova published her fourth collection, *Plantain*, and the following year she published *Anno Domini MCMXXI*, soon after which the futurist poet Vladimir Mayakovsky denounced her. The party determined not to arrest her as long as she did not publish further works.

Akhmatova continued writing, however, despite the authorities' harassment. Over the next few years she would experience chronic ill health and see her good friends the Mandelshtams exiled to Cherdyn and, in 1934, her own son arrested. In 1937–1938, the years millions of Russians were imprisoned and sent to concentration camps, her son was again arrested and held for seventeen months in Leningrad; Mandelshtam was arrested and died in a transit camp. In 1940 the ban on Akhmatova's works was briefly lifted, and *From Six Books*, a selection with new poems from her previous books, was published and then withdrawn from sale. Akhamatova suffered her first heart attack. Lev was arrested again in 1949, in part because of her 1946 meeting with Isaiah Berlin, First Secretary in the British Embassy in Moscow, and would not be released until 1956. Over the next two decades other books, *Selected Poems, Poems 1909-1945,* and *Poems 1909-1960* appeared in censored editions. Not until 1963 did an uncensored collection, *Requiem* (published in Munich), appear. Akhamatova died in a Moscow convalescent home on March 5, 1966.

BOOKS OF POETRY:

Vecher (St. Petersburg: Guild of Poets, 1912); *Chetki* (St. Petersburg: Izdatelstvo Giperborey, 1914); *Belaya staya* (St. Petersburg: Izdatelstvo Giperborey, 1917); *Skrizhal Sbornik* (1918); *U Samago Morya* (St. Petersburg: Alkonost, 1921); *Podorozhnik* (St. Petersburg: Petropolis Printers, 1921); *Anno Domini* MCMXXI (St.Petersburg: Petropolis Printers, 1921); *Stikhi* (1940); *Iz shesti knig* [censored] (Moscow: Izdatelstvo Sovetskii Pisatel, 1940); *Izbrannie Stikhi* [censored] (Tashkent, 1943); *Tashkentskie Stikhi* [censored] (Tashkent, 1944); *Izbrannie Stikhotvoreniya* (New York: Chekova, 1952); *Stikhotvoreniya 1909–1957* [censored; almost completely destroyed] Moscow: Izdatelstvo Khudozhestvennaya Literatura, 1958); *Stikhotvoreniya (Poems)* [censored] (Moscow, 1958); *Stikhi, 1909–1960* (1961); *Stikhotvoreniya 1909–1960* [censored] (Moscow, 1961); *50 Stikhotvorenii* (Paris: YMCA Press, 1963); *Rekviem: Tsikl Stikhotvorenii* (Frankfurt am Main: Possev-Verlag, 1964); *Poeziya* (Vilnyus Vaga, 1964); *Beg vremeni* [less censored] (Moscow: Izdatelstvo Sovetskii Pisatel, 1965); *Stikhotvoreniya, 1909–1965* (Moscow, 1965); *Sochineniya* [2 volumes] (Washington, DC: Inter-Language Literary Associates, 1965, 1968); *Tainy remesla* (1986); *Sochineniya v dvukh tomakh* (Khudozhestvennaya Literatura, 1986).

ENGLISH LANGUAGE TRANSLATIONS:

Forty-Seven Love Poems, translated by Natalie Doddington (London: Jonathan Cape, 1927); *Selected Poems,* translated by Richard McKane (Harmondsworth, England: Penguin, 1969); reprinted (London: Bloodaxe, 1989); *Poems of Akhmatova,* translated by Stanley Kunitz and Max Hayward (New York: Little, Brown, 1973); *A Poem Without a Hero,* translated by Carl R. Proffer and Assya Humesky (Ann Arbor, Michigan: Ardis Press, 1973); *Moscow Trefoil* (Canberra: Australian National University Press, 1975); *Requiem* [and] *Poem Without a Hero,* trans. by D. M. Thomas (Athens: Ohio University Press, 1976); *Selected Poems,* translated by Carl R. Proffer, Robin Kemball, and Walter Arndt (Ann Arbor, Michigan: Ardis Press, 1976); *The White Flock,* edited by Geoffrey Thurley (Oasis Books, 1978); *Way of All the Earth,* translated by D. M. Thomas (Athens: Ohio University Press, 1979); *Three Russian Women Poets,* translated by Mary Maddock (Freedom, California: The Crossing Press, 1983); *Poems,* translated by Lyn Coffin (New York: Norton, 1983); *You Will Hear Thunder,* translated by D. M. Thomas (Athens: Ohio University Press, 1985); *Twenty Poems* (Eighties Press/Ally Press, 1985); *Northern Elegies* (Firefly Press, 1985); *Selected Poems,* translated by D.M. Thomas (London and New York: Penguin, 1988); *The Complete Poems of Anna Akhmatova,* translated by Judith Hemschemeyer (Boston: Zephyr Press and Edinburgh: Canongate Press, 1992).

In my room lives a beautiful
Slow black snake;
It is like me, just as lazy,
Just as cold.

In the evening I compose marvelous tales
On the rug by the fire's red glow,
And with emerald eyes
It gazes at me indifferently.

At night the dead, mute icons hear
Resisting moans...
It's true, I would desire another
Were it not for the serpent eyes.

But in the morning, submissive once more, I
Melt, like a slender candle...
And then from my bare shoulder
A black ribbon slides.

—Translated from the Russian by Judith Hemschemeyer

1910 [uncollected]

He Loved...

He loved three things in life:
Evensong, white peacocks
And old maps of America.
He hated it when children cried,
He hated tea with raspberry jam
And women's hysterics.
...And I was his wife.

—Translated from the Russian by Judith Hemschemeyer

1910, Kiev
(from *Vecher*, 1912)

I don't need legs anymore,
Let them turn into a fish's tail!
I'm swimming and the coolness is delightful,
The far-off bridge grows dimly white.

I don't need a submissive soul,
Let it turn into smoke, a wisp of smoke
Of tender, light blue
Flying over the blackened quay.

See how deeply I dive,
Clutching seaweed in my hands,
No one's words will I repeat
And no one's longing will capture me...

But you, my distant one, is it true
That you've become sadly mute and pale?
What's this I hear? That for three whole weeks
You've been whispering: "Why, unhappy girl?"

—Translated from the Russian by Judith Hemschemeyer

1911
(from *Vecher,* 1912)

She approached. I didn't betray my agitation,
Just stared serenely out the window.
She sat there, like a porcelain idol,
In a pose she had adopted long ago.

Being cheerful—becomes a habit,
Being attentive—is more difficult...
Or has languorous indolence triumphed
After those heady March nights?

The tiresome buzz of conversation,
The lifeless heat of the yellow chandelier,
And over the slightly raised, slender arm,
The glimpse of an artful coiffure.

Her companion smiles again
And watches her hopefully...
My lucky, rich inheritor,
Welcome to my legacy.

—Translated from the Russian by Judith Hemschemeyer

1914
(from *Belaya staya*, 1917)

It's impossible to get here
By either rowboat or cart,
The water stands deep
On the rotten snow,
Besieging the estate
On all sides...
Ah! Nearby pines
A sort of Robinson Crusoe.
He walks around staring at sleighs,
At horses, at skis,
And then he sits on the divan
And waits for me,
Shredding the carpet
With his short spurs.
Now that meek smile
Won't appear in the mirrors.

—Translated from the Russian by Judith Hemschemeyer

1916, Slepnyovo
(from *Belaya staya*, 1917)

To the Beloved

Don't send me a dove,
Don't write me disquieting letters,
Don't make the March wind keen in my face.
Yesterday I entered green paradise,
Where there is peace for body and soul
Under a tent of the poplars' shadow.

And from here I see the little city,
The barracks and sentry boxes at the palace,
The yellow Chinese bridge above the ice.
For three hours you've been awaiting me—you waver,
But you cannot leave the porch
And you marvel, so many new stars.

As a gray squirrel, I will leap on the alder tree,
As a weasel, shy, I'll scurry by,
As a swan, I'll call to you,
So that it won't be terrible for the groom
To wait in the whirling blue snow
For his dead bride.

—*Translated from the Russian by Judith Hemschemeyer*

1915, Tsarskoye Selo
(from *Belaya Staya*, 1917)

So, I remained alone,
Counting the empty days.
O, my free companions,
My swans!

And I'll not summon you with song,
Not bring you back with tears,
But in the sad hour of dusk,
Remember you in my prayers.

Struck by the deadly arrow,
One of you has fallen,
And another, kissing me,
Has become a black raven.

But it happens, once a year
When the ice is melting,
I stand by the clear waters
In the Catherine Gardens.

And I hear the splashing of great wings
Over the blue surface of the lake.
I do not know who has opened the window
In the prison of the grave.

—Translated from the Russian by Daniel Weissbort

1917
(from *Podorozhnik*, 1921)

A monstrous rumor roams the city,
Stealing into houses, like a thief.
Shouldn't I read the story of Bluebeard
Before I lie down to sleep?

How the seventh bride mounted the staircase,
How she called to her younger sister,
She waited—holding her breath,
For her dear brothers or the dreaded messenger...

A snowy cloud of dust flies,
The brothers dash into the castle courtyard,
And over the tender and innocent neck
The slippery ax will not rise.

Now, comforted by this fairy tale,
I'll certainly sleep peacefully.
Why then is my heart pounding,
Why can't I close my eyes?

—Translated from the Russian by Judith Hemschemeyer

1921
(from *Anno Domini* MCMXXI, 1921)

The Poet

He who compared himself to the eye of a horse,
He glances sideways, looks, sees, recognizes,
And instantly puddles shine
As melted diamonds, ice pines.

In lilac haze repose backyards,
Station platforms, logs, leaves, clouds.
The whistle of a steam engine, the crunch of watermelon rind,
In a fragrant kid glove, a timid hand.

He rings out, thunders, grates, he beats like the surf
And suddenly grows quiet—it means that he
Is cautiously advancing through the pines,
So as not to disturb the light sleep of space.

And it means that he is counting the grains
From the stripped stalks, it means that he
Has come back to a Daryal gravestone, cursed and black,
After some kind of funeral.

And once more, Moscow weariness burns the throat,
Far off, a deadly little bell is ringing...
Who lost his way two steps from the house,
Up to the waist in snow and no way out?

Because he compared smoke to the Laocoon,
and celebrated cemetery thistles,
Because he filled the world with the new sound
Of his verse reverberating in new space—

He was rewarded with a kind of eternal childhood,
His generosity and keen-sightedness shone,
The whole earth was his inheritance,
And he shared it with everyone.

—*Translated from the Russian by Judith Hemschemeyer*

(from *Iz Shesti Knig*, 1940)

from *Sweetbrier in Blossom: From a Burnt Notebook*

9
In a Broken Mirror

That starry night I heard
Irretrievable words,
And my head whirled
As if over a flaming abyss.
And destruction howled at the door,
And the black garden echoed like an eagle owl,
And the city, mortally weakened,
Was Troy at that ancient hour.
That hour was unbearably clear
And, it seemed, it reverberated to the point of tears.
The gift you gave me
Was not brought from afar.
It seemed to you idle diversion
On that fiery night.
And it became slow poison
In my enigmatic fate.
And it was the forerunner of all my misfortunes—
Let's not remember it!..
Still sobbing around the corner is
The meeting that never took place.

—Translated from the Russian by Judith Hemschemeyer

1956
(from *Beg Vremeni*, 1965)

PERMISSIONS

["In my room lives a beautiful"], "He Loved...," ["She approached. I didn't betray my agitation,"], ["It's impossible to get here"], "To the Beloved," ["A Monstrous rumor roams the city,"], "The Poet," and "9 / In a Broken Mirror,"
Reprinted from *The Complete Poems of Anna Akhmatova*, trans. by Judith Hemschemeyer, and Edited by Roberta Reeder (Boston: Zephyr Press and Edinburgh: Canongate Press, 1992). ©1990, 1992 by Judith Hemschemeyer. Reprinted by permission of Zephyr Press.

["So, I remained alone"]
Reprinted from *Twentieth-Century Russian Poetry*, Edited by John Glad and Daniel Weissbort, trans. by Daniel Weissbort (Iowa City: University of Iowa Press, 1992). ©1992 by the University of Iowa Press. Reprinted by permission of the University of Iowa Press.

[José] Oswald de [Souza] Andrade [Brazil]
1890–1954

Andrade in 1919

Born in São Paulo in 1890, Andrade was the son of a wealthy family whose business was in coffee. In 1912 he visted Paris, coming under the influence of F.T. Marinetti's Futurist writings. On his return to Brazil he studied law, and received his degree in 1919. But over these years, he increasingly involved himself with writers and artists, and sought to rebel against the traditional society of Brazilian culture. In 1920, he founded the magazine *Papel e tinta*, and with other young poets and critics organized the Week of Modern Art in São Paulo in 1922, which is said to have been the beginning of Brazilian modernism.

In 1923, Andrade published his first important work, the novel *Memórias sentimentais de João Miramar (The Sentimental Memoirs of João Miramar)*, a book written in a telegraphic style similar to that he had discovered in the Italian Futurists. The fragmentation of the narrative into brief chapters, the numerous puns and linguistic associations, and the poetic style and diction have also brought critics to compare the book with the work of James Joyce.

A second trip to Paris solidified his involvement in the avant garde, and in 1925 he published *Pau Brasil* (Brazilwood), in which he propounded the ideas of "primitive" writing free of the influences of other languages and cultures, and a discarding of meter and rhyme, all of which were to become the foundations of the Brazilian modernist movement. In a manifesto of 1928, *Anthropological Manifesto*, Andrade further developed his aesthetic doctrine, with its emphasis on cultural cannibalism and the native language. In it he continued his advocation of a return to the primitive and an eschewing of European influences.

His second important fiction, *Serafim Ponte Grade*, was written during the 1930 revolution that brought Getulio Vargas to power, and helped to make Andrade aware of the brutal realities of Brazilian life. His preface to that book satirizes some of his modernist friends and denounces his own participation in the movement. Henceforward, Andrande refocused his literary activities on social commitment.

Andrade also published plays such as the 1937 *O rei da vela* and numerous books of poetry, collected in 1945 *Poesias reunidas*. He died in 1954, completely out of tune with the modernism he had help to create.

BOOKS OF POETRY:

Memórias sentimentais de João Miramar (1924 [mixed genre]); *Pau Brasil* (1925); *Primeiro Caderno do Aluno de Poesia Oswald de Andrade* (1927); *Poesias reunidas* (1945).

ENGLISH LANGUAGE TRANSLATIONS:

Sentimental Memoirs of John Seaborne, translated by Ralph Niebuhr and Albert Bork in *The Texas Quarterly*, xv, no. 4, p. 112+.

from *Sentimental Memoirs of João Miramar*

Sorrento

Crones sails cicadas
Mists on the Vesuvian sea
Geckoed gardens and golden women
Between walls of garden-path grapes
Of lush orchards
Piedigrotta insects
Gnawing matchboxes in the trousers pocket
White trigonometries
In the blue crepe of Neapolitan waters
Distant city siestas quiet
Amidst scarves thrown over the shoulder
Dotting indigo grays of hillocks

   An old Englishman slept with his mouth open
like the blackened mouth of a tunnel beneath civilized
eyeglasses.
   Vesuvius awaits eruptive orders from Thomas Cook & Son.
   And a woman in yellow informed a sport-shirted individual
that marriage was an unbreakable contract.

Sal o May

The cabarets of São Paulo are remote
As virtues

Automobiles
And the intelligent signal lights of the roads
One single soldier to police my entire homeland
And the cru-cru of the crickets creates bagpipes
And the toads talk twaddle to easy lady toads
In the obscure alphabet of the swamps
Vowels
Street lamps night lamps
And you appear through a clumsy and legendary fox trot

Delenda lovely Salomé
Oh tawdry dancing girl
Full of ignorant flies and good intentions

The *javá* is a piggish polka with blue dust
But the purple empurples the procession of pink curtains

"I don't give a damn."
"I want to know about that nonsense of waiting with
the revolver on the road."
"That black thug gave her a punch and the woman took
a kick."
"In her belly."
The saxophone persists in an ache of frenzied teeth
Which the maxixe spasms
Between shots and tips
But the open leakage of gas escapes
Into the penitentiary night
"Lord grant us the illumined spongecake of redemption"

The Tieté rolls heaps of bricks
Water-colored and pink.

—*Translated from the Portuguese by Jack E. Tomlins*

(from *Memórias sentimentais de João Miramar, 1924*)

Babbling

Cabralism. The civilization of the donées. The Willing and
the Exportation.
The Carnival. The Hinterland and the Slum.
Brazilwood. Barbaric and ours.

The rich ethnic formation. The richness of the vegetation.
The minerals. The food. The vatapá, the gold and the dance.

All history of Penetration and the commerical history of America.
Brazilwood.

Against the fatality of the first white man who entered the port
and diplomatically dominated the savage jungles. Citing Virgil to the
Tupiníquím people. The bachelor.

Country of anonymous pains. Of anonymous doctors. Society of erudite
shipwrecked people.

From where the never exportation of poetry. The poetry tangled in the culture. In the lianas of the versifications.

Twentieth century. A burst in the learning. The men who knew everything were deformed like rubber babels. They burst free of encyclopaedism.

The poetry for the poets. Happiness of the ignorance that discovers. Pedr'Alvares.

The suggestion from Blaise Cendrars:—You have the locomotives full, you leave. A black man turns the handle of the rotary where you are. The smallest carelessness will make you leave, in a direction opposite to that of your destiny.

Against cabinetism, the tramping of the climates.

The language without archaisms. Without erudition. Natural and neo-logic. The millionaire contribution of all of the mistakes.

From naturalism one had passed to domestic pyrography and to the excursionist kodak.

All the girls talented. Virtuosos of the player piano.
The processions went out of the bulge of the factories.
It was necessary to un-do. Deformation through impressionism and the symbol. The lyricism brand-new. The presentation of the materials.

The coincidence of the first Brazilian construction in the movement of general reconstruction. Brazilwood poetry.

Against the naturalistic subtlety, the synthesis. Against the copy, the invention and the surprise.

A perspective of an order other than visual. The correspondent to the physical miracle in art. Closed stars in the photographic negatives.

And the wise solar laziness. The prayer. The silent energy. The hospitality.

Barbaric, picturesque and credulous. Brazilwood. The forest and the school. The food, the minerals and the dance. The vegetation. Brazilwood.

—Translated from the Portuguese by Flavia Vidal

(*Pau-Brasil*, 1925)

Portuguese Mistake

When the Portuguese came
In a heavy rain
He dressed the Indian.
Pity!
If it had been a sunny morning
The Indian would have stripped
The Portuguese.

—*Translated from the Portuguese by Régis Bonvicino
and Douglas Messerli*

(Pau-Brasil, 1925)

Epitaph

I am round, round
Round, round I know
I am a round island
Of the women I have kissed

Because I died for oh! love
Of the women of my island
My skull will laugh ha ha ha
Thinking of the roundel

—*Translated from the Portuguese by Jean R. Longland*

Ballad of the Esplanade Hotel

Late last night
I tried
To see if I
Could write
A ballad
Before I got
To my hotel

Long ago
This heart

Had enough
Of life alone
And wants
To stay with you
At the Esplanade

I wished
I could
Cover this paper
With lovely phrases
It's so good
To be
A minstrel

In future
The generations
Passing this way
Will say
It's the hotel
of the minstrel

For inspiration
I open windows
Like magazines
I must construct
The ballad
Of the Esplanade
And end up
Being the minstrel
Of my hotel

But there's no
Poetry in hotels
Even though
They're Grand Hotels
Or Esplanades

There's poetry
In hibiscus
In the hummingbird
In the traitor
In the elevator

(Envoy)

Who knows what
If some day
The elevator
Would bring
Your love
Up here

—*Translated from the Portuguese by Thomas Colchie*

Good Luck

Four hundred years ago
you landed in the Tropic of Capricorn
on the carbuncular plank
of ships
steered by dark stars
the pale beetle
of the seas
Every exile was a king
skinny, insomniac, colorless
as clay

You will create a world
from coarse laughter
from sterile glues
from coarse laughter
You will plant insurgent hatreds side by side
frustrated hatreds
You will evoke humanity, mist and frost
Among the lianas you will build a palace of termites
and from a tower circled by hills
bleating with sincere cincerre-bells
you will rise toward the moon
like hope

Space is a prison.

—*Translated from the Portuguese by Flavia Vidal*

(*Poesias reunidas*, 1945)

Ece Ayhan [Turkey]
1931

Ece Ayhan

The poet Ece Ayhan Çağlar was born in 1931 in the western province of Turkey, Muğla, on the Aegean sea. He attended elementary and secondary schools at the Atatürk Lycée in Istanbul; he then attended the school of Political Sciences in the capital city of Ankara, graduating in 1959. From 1962 to 1966, Ece Ayhan was a civil servant, a head district administrator (*kaymakam*) in the Anatolian districts of Gurun, Alaca and Cardak. In 1966 he quit his position. Returning to Istanbul, he worked as a translator for the Turkish edition of the French dictionary *Larousse (Meydan Larousse)* and the archives section of Turkish Cinematèque Association. Since 1966 he has held no other job.

By 1966 Ayhan had already written two of his three major works, *Kinar Hanimin Denizleri* ("Miss Kinar's Waters") (1959) and *Bakissiz Bir Kedi Kara (A Blind Cat Black)* (1965). To write his third, *Orthodoxies* (1968), his most historical, satirical, fact- and Istanbul-obsessed work—a pun filled, vertical serialism—Ece Ayhan moved to the streets of Istanbul. The poem delves into the underbelly of the city, Galata, historically both its red light district—of transvestites, girl and boy prostitutes, tattooed roughs, and heroin merchants, that is, the unnamed or "euphemized" outcasts of Turkish culture—and the district where minorities—Armenians, Greeks, Jews, Russians, etc.—lived.

Since 1968, Ayhan has published *State and Nature* (1973) and *Disperse and Move Out of the Way (1977)*, a collection of his work until 1976 with essays on him, and several other books.

BOOKS OF POETRY:

Kinar Hanimin Denizleri (Istanbul, 1959); *Bakissiz Bir Kedi Kara* (Istanbul, 1965); *Ortodoksluklar* (Istanbul, 1968); *Devlet Ve Tabiat* (Istanbul, 1968); *Yurt Savul* [poems and essays on the poet] (Istanbul, 1977, 1982, 1993); *Zambakli Padisah* (Ankara, 1981); *Cok Eski Adiyladir* (Istanbul, 1982); *Yanliz Kardesce* (Eski Sehir, 1984); *Kolsuz Bir Hattat* (Istanbul, 1987); *Canakkaleli Melahata Iki El Mektup* [prose poems] (Istanbul, 1991); *Son Siirler* (Istanbul, 1993).

ENGLISH LANGUAGE TRANSLATIONS:

A Blind Cat Black and *Orthodoxies*, translated by Murat Nemet-Nejat (Los Angeles: Sun & Moon Press, 1997).

Miss Kinar's Waters

She cried the smile of pebble stones with the raki from the carafe
from Miss Kinar now who became water to steep wells
with her straight hair what can she do in the theatre houses of Shehzadebashi
she could not have enough hats

This bald Hassan, this baldie swept the darkness
his rebellious cigarette lit backwards to avoid any laughter
and a police enters fairy tales which go on ever since
parting the human eyelashes of children

And gathered inside her the sadness of the hands of an oud
playing woman, appeared suddenly into wells in the evenings crying
from Miss Kinar's waters

—*Translated from the Turkish by Murat Nemet-Nejat*

(from *Kinar Hanimin Denizleri,* 1959)

The Nigger in the Photograph

Accursed. The curse which with its curving unsheathed letter will never leave me alone, which I take everywhere, my invisible dog, the curse. Who can be friends with me? Who? It is rumored I carry that monk's blood, and with a relentless agitation I run here and there, barefoot, and on my tiny chin a big beauty spot, I am known with my covered beauty still. Like the stain in the curve of the letter *U*.

Flower. I began my adventures as a flower vender. Flowers and children bedecking a string, dry petals. But how I was under a spell those days. Because of a little fairy's curse, I couldn't be looked at. Light Maltese fevers run in empty lots in summer evenings. And endless hallucinations full of clowns run in ruins. Then a stone arched passage. I am living in the drawer of a fifty-year-old witch, nailed. Am I really? One can not tell what season it is, and I am cold. Curved like the letter *U*.

...I went to Jerusalem in that exile of the flower vendors and got settled in the town clock... But to remember these things, I don't want to remember them... It had run out, the money I had saved selling flowers... This far away from Smyrna, I was pawned. Let this be the nigger in the negative of a photograph from me, will you receive it one day? I had it taken while learning Hebrew, with my invisible dog inside a Jewess. Lonely and terrible. Under a huge tree which had shed its leaves, barely touching a chair.

It is not out of pity, but I am worried it won't pass. The curve of the letter *U*.

—*Translated from the Turkish by Murat Nemet-Nejat*

(from *Bakissiz Bir Kedi Kara,* 1965)

The Secret Jew

Lidless, one of the devils, he is pulling out with my streetcar money. From time to time, going downtown like this, I feel sad and shaky. In the hotel I sleep in his (my Corpse's) bed. When his hair keeps growing jet black like that what is it that my live body begrudges and I try to give to him. With my large beefy hands. A sharp spur. Odor of sulphur. A scarred copper-branded ass. In the sewers of my veins, there, a rat. It nibbles at the town and the hanging tree in me. Crazies, rats, male rats, share (you must share, children) a charred corpse. In the cellar. There were no little words of loving him, these keys on his belt (warden, lover!) couldn't be little cooing words of loving him. I ran away, scared, not to meet the porcelain doll. To meet him. That would be my going back to the Lexicon of Torture. The widow plant of the idiot forests eating up joy, the poppy hatred of seven years, the silk hand with cowhide gloves doling out inheritance. He doesn't want to be buried, he says. He is cold. On the back platform of the streetcar the young devil on fire disappearing. I am picking out my spectacles from the swamps of my envy. After the arsonist's fire the brother of my Ex-Mistress (my Corpse) who disappeared. He can be recognized by the delicate insect-eyed family mask covering his coarse face. That guy. Why should I sob anyway. He loves easily, passes his hand below the belt of my vault, forgets easily what a secret Jew I am.

—*Translated from the Turkish by Murat Nemet-Nejat*

(from *Bakissiz Bir Kedi Kara*, 1965)

The Blue Bead, Against the Evil Eye

Madness put on a porkpie hat. He ran to the regions where sellers of guns go bankrupt. Founded the empire of truants. And, then, found a golden cannonball in the town of Monastery.

Pinned on his collar a forest in September. No one should know of the secret treasure full of trinkets. The hyena was there, too, with the face of a rotten apple. He fought madly to grab the dagger.

There was talk one Saturday of the Crimea. Wars. The sorcery stores were closed. They hanged him inside a liquor bottle, heavy silver boots on his feet, smiling. Against all sorts of jinx. This little, vagabond imp.

—*Translated from the Turkish by Murat Nemet-Nejat*

(from *Bakissiz Bir Kedi Kara*, 1965)

A Blind Cat Black

An absent-mided tightrope walker comes. From the sea of late hours. Blows out a
lamp. Lies down next to my weeping side, for the sake of the prophet. A blind woman
downstairs. Family. She raves in a language I don't know. On her chest a heavy butterfly,
broken drawers in it. My Aunt Sadness drinks alcohol in the attic, embroiders. Ex-
pelled from many schools. A blind cat passes in the the black street. In its sack a child
just dead. His wings don't fit, too big. The Old Hawker cries. A pirate ship. Has entered
the port.

—*Translated from the Turkish by Murat Nemet-Nejat*

(from *Bakissiz Bir Kedi Kar*, 1965)

Orthodoxies I

His only side—his face—to be talked about: the space between his legs. And he has
grown a moustache and a beard. An inveterate. A pervert. Such talk about him. He
doesn't go near women as he should. He whets suspicion. An erect plume on his head.
A barber's piece. A pornographic masterpiece. He is buried alive in the ground. Head
first. Ouch! A few sailboats, startled, shine at a distance. Why couldn't I understand?

Modesty, a mood. Shame is held delicately by the hand. A girl, blighted. Walks
under the eaves of her man. The door locks have given in by themselves. A shroud
moves. She has grown pregnant by leaning over the corpse. Which pretends impo-
tence in a church. Before it tends. She has reared the foundling in the marshes. I was
burning a blank letter by pouring gasoline on it. A con man's envelope on the side-
walk. Shining beeswax. Melts.

Now, a leftover. Know. The bend in a child's heart. His crafty, elegant wrist. And
how he holds a hawk, stuffed, whole, trying to preen its feathers. He has written etched
over his breast in saffron repeating, embroidering one word from the lexicon end-
lessly: hermaphrodite. A hermetic woman. A thief woman. A thief of she. He makes
love biting her own lip. He plays the hand-me-down tune on the lute. Of the scared. I
was reading *The Jew of Malta*. I took shelter in a coffin.

—*Translated from the Turkish by Murat Nemat-Nejat*

(from *Ortodoksluklar*, 1968)

Orthodoxies III

What is it saying, I wonder, the purl and stitch scarf of the boy, dancing, the silk embroidery? A bird with four legs and the face of a flower.

And a wooden pestle, dipping, dipping into his sleep of cistern rain waters. By dint of precious habit.

Let them whistle the warped tune. His soapy earrings, a lewd bathroom ditty. And, now, a tambourine and its cymbals—his music tools—dropped, lie by the side.

Altered horses are raced in every neighborhood. The face painting* of a virgin bride melts away to the depths of a metamorphosis.

—*Translated from the Turkish by Murat Nemat-Nejat*

(from *Ortodoksluklar*, 1968)

Orthodoxies XV

A crack of lilacs. A mask chipped off their wood. It is impenetrably wide, he understands.

Kneeling, he groans, one Benjamin. Weaned off the smell of armpits. A cup of hemlock not left around against the possibility of drink.

And there is a majolica on the mat. A fortress tower rings, of the harem's eunuches, washed in the flood.

Screaming, under a parasol, he adorns the portable throne. In a blackout. In his birthday suit.

And a slut is giving him a broken tipped sword. Reveals herself on the rung of a ladder. Oh, Benjamin!

Two snakes entwined, trajectories melting away at an inn. Turned around by so many bends.

In the guise of an eagle owl, bubo-bubo, the fallen Christ** goes out to paint the town red. And he won't come back.

*In villages the paint on the bride's face is a symbol of her virginity.
**Russian belief that, in the shape of a beggar, Christ will cross Russia one day. The Russians wait for him. He wanders now in the cities at night disguised as a large owl, bubo-bubo.

—*Translated from the Turkish by Murat Nemat-Nejat*

(from *Ortodoksluklar*, 1965)

Gottfried Benn [Germany]
1886–1956

Gottfried Benn

The son of a Lutheran minister and a mother of French-Swiss extraction, Gottfried Benn was raised in the small German village of Mansfeld, in an area which is now part of Poland. There he was educated privately and in the Gymnasium at Frankfurt an der Order, living in the same boarding-house as did the poet Klabund. In 1903, following his father's desires, he entered the University of Marbach, studying theology and philosophy. But he soon switched to medicine at the Kaiser Wilhelm Akademie, a part of the University of Berlin, and, upon graduating, focused on venereolgy and dermatology as a medical doctor until the end of World War I.

In 1912, upon his graduation from medical school Benn was called to active military duty, but fell ill from the strenuous training. During this period, in utter mental and physical exhaustion, he wrote the work *Morgue und andere Gedichte* (Morgue and Other Poems), which focuses on the kind of haunted visions and depersonalization of contemporary man that characterized much of Expressionist writing. The reaction to his poems, filled with drug-addicts, prostitutes, alcoholics, and other low-life figures, was one of outrage from bourgeois readers. During this period he met and entered into an intimate relationship with the poet Else Lasker-Schüler, and dedicated his second book, *Söhne* (published in 1913) to her.

Upon discharge from the military, Benn became employed as an assistant at the Pathological Institute of Westend Hospital, where he performed hundreds of autopsies. As a result of this employment and the mental anguish from which he suffered and expressed in his poetry, he left that position, becoming a ship's physician in the spring of 1913. However, Benn suffered from sea-sickness, and, in New York, left the ship, attending a performance of Enrico Caruso at the Metropolitan Opera, and ultimately returning to Berlin. The ship to which he was to have been assigned sank with no survivors.

His third collection of poetry, *Fleisch* (Flesh), was published in 1917. This book carried further his prevailing sentiments of melancholy and cynicism. Over the next several years, his poetry continued to appear in expressionist journals, where he came to be recognized as a major avant-garde writer. But his work continued to move toward Nietzschean ideas that saw art as an escape from nihilism and sought, as solace to the suffering of mankind, beliefs underlying ancient mythologies and their primal urges. In 1916 Benn published a collection of short tales, *Gehirne* (Brains) which explored the psyche and its pulls between the Dionysian and Apollonian elements, ideas which he would further develop in his 1920 essay *Das moderne Ich* (The Modern Self).

These ideas, popular in their day, at first seemed simply to be a part of his unorthodox poetics; but with the rise of National Socialism, which shared many of these underlying beliefs, it became apparent that Benn was on a dangerous intellectual path. In the late 1920s and early

1930s he greeted Hitler's rise to power enthusiastically, expressing his shared values of the Nazi eugenics program and other concepts of the "German folk" on radio and in essays. Several of his Expressionist friends, now in exile in Russia and elsewhere, reproached him, further isolating his from the literary avant-garde. With Hitler's appointment to the head of German government in 1933, Heinrich Mann, the president of the literary academy, called for the Socialist-Communist coalition to overthrow Hitler. Benn supported Hitler, and Mann and his brother Thomas were expelled and, ultimately, forced to leave the country. Klaus Mann and others now questioned Benn's cooperation with Hitler's regime. Benn fought back through radio speeches. But he soon was himself denounced as a Jew, and was forbidden a health certificate to practice medicine. When his new collection, *Ausegwählte Gedichte* was published in 1936, in celebration of his fiftieth birthday, the book was denounced by the SS newspaper *Das Schwarze Korps* and was reprinted in Nazi journals. In 1938 he was officially ousted from his membership in the Reichsschrifttumskammer and threatened with penalties if he continued writing.

After the War, Benn was further attacked by figures such as Bertolt Brecht and Alfred Döblin for his involvement with the Nazi regime. But he still had many friends, and with their support and the publication of his collection *Statische Gedichte* (Static Poems, 1948) and his lengthy autobiographical essay *Doppelleben* (Double Life) in 1950, he began to rehabilitate his career. In 1961 he won the Georg Büchner Prize of Poetry, upon which he delivered his famous essay, *Probleme der Lyrik* (Problems for Poetry). His final volumes, *Destillationen* (Distillations, 1953) and *Apréslude* (Afterlude, 1955) continued the expression of despair and disillusionment of his major poetry. Today Benn is recognized as one of the greatest of German poets, perhaps the best since Rilke.

BOOKS OF POETRY:

Morgue und andere Gedichte (Berlin-Wilmersdorf: Meyer, 1912); *Söhne: Neue Gedichte* (Berlin-Wilmersdorf, 1913); *Fleisch: Gesammelte Lyrik* (Berlin-Wilmersdorf: Aktion, 1917); *Betäubung: Fünf neue Gedichte* (Berlin-Wilmersdorf: Meyer, 1925); *Spaltung: Neue Gedichte* (Berlin: Meyer, 1925); *Das Unaufhörliche: Oratorim* [text by Benn, music by Paul Hindemith (Mainz: Schott, 1931); *Zweiundzwanzig Gedichte: 1936-1943* (Berlin: privately printed, 1953); *Statische Gedichte* (Zurich: Arche, 1948); *Fragmente: Neue Gedichte* (Weisbaden: Limes, 1951); *Destillationen: Neue Gedichte* (Weisbaden: Limes, 1953); *Apréslude* (Weisbaden: Limes, 1955); *Gesammelte Gedichte 1912-1956* (Wiesbaden: Limes, 1956); *Gesammelte Werke in vier Bänden. Band 3: Gedichte* (Wiesbaden: Limes, 1959-1961).

ENGLISH LANGUAGE TRANSLATIONS:

Selected Poems (London: Oxford Press, 1970); *Primal Vision: Selected Writings of Gottfried Benn*, edited by E. B. Ashton (New York: New Directions, 1971); *Gottfried Benn: Prose, Essays, Poems*, edited by Volkmar Sander (New York: Continuum, 1987).

Poplar

Restrained,
with branch and young shoot undisclosed
to cry the louder out into the blue of sky—:
trunk only, all enclosure,
tall and shivering,
a curve.

Medlar is fugitive,
killer of seed,
and when have blessing clefts of lightning
roared round my shaft,
disuniting,
casting far and wide
the thing once tree?
Who ever saw a wood of poplars?

Individual
restless at night and through the day
over the gardens' mignonetted
sweet deliquescence gaping wide
that sucks its root and gnaws its bark
insignia of cries on its crowned brow it offers
dead space opposing,
to and fro

—Translated from the German by Christopher Middleton

(from *Fleisch*, 1917)

Palau

"Evening is red on the island of Palau
and the shadows sink—"
sing, from woman's chalices too
it is good to drink,
deathly the little owls cry
and the death-watch ticks out,
very soon it will be
Lemures and night.

Hot these reefs. From eucalypti there flows
a tropical palm concoction,
all that still holds and stays
also longs for destruction
down to the limbless stage,
down to the vacuum,
back to the primal age,
dark ocean's womb.

Evening is red on the island of Palau:
in the gleam of these shadows
these issues rising from twilight and dew:
"Never and Always";
all the deaths of the earth
are fords and ferries,
what to you owes it birth
surrounded with strangeness—

Once with sacrificial
fat on the pine-wood floor
your bed of flames would travel
like wine to the shore,
megaliths heaped around
and the graves and the halls,
hammer of Thor that's bound
for the Aesir, crumbled, falls—

As the gods surcease,
the great Caesars decline,
from the cheek of Zeus
once raised up to reign—
sing, already the world
to the strangest rhythm is swung,
Charon's coin, if not curled,
long tasted under the tongue—

Coupling. Sepias your seas
and coral animate,
all that still holds and sways
also longs to disintegrate,
evening is red on the island of Palau,
eucalyptus glaze

raises in runes from twilight and dew:
Never and Always.

—*Translated from the German by Michael Hamburger*

(from *Spaltung: Neue Gedichte*, 1925)

Monologue

Their colons fed with mucus, brains with lies
these chosen races, coxcombs of a clown,
in pranks, astrology and flight of birds
construing their own ordure! Slaves—
from icy and from burning territories,
gross with vermin more and more slaves come,
hungry and whiplash-driven hordes of them:
Then all that's personal, the downy cheek,
with scurf and scab, swells to a prophet's beard!

Ah, Alexander and Olympia's offspring,
that least of all! They wink whole Hellesponts,
and skim all Asia! Puffed up, pustules
with vanguard, covert squadrons and with minions
that none may prick them! Minions: the best seats
for wrestling and in court! Let no man prick them!
Minions, joyriders, bandages, broad streamers—
broad streamers fluttering from dream and world:
the clubfoot sees the stadiums destroyed,
skunks trample underfoot the lupin fields
because the scent makes them suspect their own:
Nothing but excrement! The obese
course after the gazelle,
the windswift one, the lovely animal!
Inverse proportion enters everything:
The puddle plumbs the source, the worm the ell,
toad squirts his liquid in the violet's mouth,
and—hallelujah!—wets his pot on stones:
The reptile horde as history's moument!
The Ptolemaic line as tic-tac language,
the rat arrives as balm against the plague.
Most foul sings murder. Gossips wheedle
obscenity from psalms.

And this earth whispers discourse with the moon,
then round its hips it hangs a Mayday feast
then lets the roses pass, then stews the corn,
forbids Vesuvius erupt, won't let the cloud
become a caustic that would prick and shrivel
the beasts' base form whose fraud contrived this state—
oh, all the play on earth of fruit and rose
is given up to evil's usury,
brain-fungus, and the gorge's speckling lies
of the above-named sort, proportion inverse!

To die means leaving all these things unsolved,
the images unsure, and hungry dreams
abandoned in the rifts between the worlds—
but action means: to serve vulgarity,
aid and abet iniquity, means loneliness
and dropping furtively the great solution
that visions are and the desire of dreams,
for gain, for gold, promotion, posthumous fame,
while giddily like a moth, indifferent
as a petard the end is near and bodes
a meaning that is different—

A sound, a curve, a chink of blue almost,
reverberated through the park one night
as I stood there—: a song,
only an outline, casual, three notes heard,
and occupied all space and made the night
so full, the garden full of apparitions,
created so the world and bedded me
prostrate within the stream of things, the sad
sublime infirmity of being's birth—:
a sound, only a curve—: but being's birth—
only a curve, proportion it restored
and comprehended all things, act and dreaming...

A garland interwined of scarlet brains
whose flowers grown from scattered fever-seed
shout to each other, keeping separate:
"the coloration form" and "edges frayed,
the last thread snapping" and "a hard cold contour,"
these spicy pickles of the protoplasm,

Here transformation starts: the beasts' base form
shall so decay the very word corruption
will smell for it too much of heaven—the vultures
are gathering now and famished hawks are poised!

—Translated from the German by Christopher Middleton

(from *Statische Gedichte*, 1948)

Chopin

Not very forthcoming in conversation,
opinions were not his forte,
opinions don't get to the center;
when Delacroix expounded a theory
he became restive, he for his part was unable
to explicate his Nocturnes.

Weak as a lover;
shadows at Nohant,
where George Sand's children
would not accept
his pedagogic advice.

Consumptive, of the kind
with hemorrhages and cicatrization,
the kind that drags on for years;
quiet death
as opposed to one
with paroxysms of pain
or one by the firing-squad:
They moved his grand piano (Erard) up to the door
and Delphine Potocka
sang for him at his dying hour
a violet song.

To England he went with three pianos:
Pleyel, Erard, Broadwood,
gave for twenty guineas
fifteen-minute recitals
at Rothschild's, the Wellingtons, at Stratford House,
and to countless garters;

darkened by weariness and approaching death,
he went home
to the Square d'Orleans.

Then he burnt his sketches
and manuscripts;
no residues please, no fragments or notes
they grant such revealing insights—
and said at the end:
"My endeavors are as complete
as it was in my power to make them."

Every finger was to play
with the force appropriate to its structure;
the fourth is the weakest
(mere siamese twin to the middle finger).
When he began they rested
on E, F sharp, G sharp, B, C.

The man who has ever heard
certain Preludes by him,
whether in country houses or
in a mountain landscape
or on a terrace, through open doors,
a sanatorium's for instance,
will hardly forget it.

Never composed an opera,
no symphony,
only these tragic progressions
out of artistic conviction
and with a slender hand.

—Translated from the German by Michael Hamburger

(from *Statische Gedichte*, 1948)

September

I

You leaning there over the fence with phlox
(splintered by rainstorm,
with a strange animal smell),
who are pleased to walk over stubble
and to accost old folk
gathering balm-apples,
breathe with joy and sadness
smoke over ploughland—

rising walls want there
roof before the snow and winter come,
to shout a "You're wasting your time"
at lime-slaking laborers,
but, hesitant, restrain yourself,

thickset rather than tall in build,
with dirty pumpkin also bare at your shoe,
fat and faceless this toady growth—

Descender from the plains,
ultimate moon of all flames,
from tumescences of fruit and flower
dropping, darkened your face already—
fool or baptist,
summer's fool, echoer, necrologue,
or foresong of glaciers,
anyway nutcracker,
sedge-cutter,
ponderer of platitudes—

Snowfall ahead of you,
high silence, barren
the far unplantable distance:
that far your reach extends,
but, leaning over the fence,
throngs of beetles and plants now,
all life-desiring things,
spiders and fieldmice—

II

You, rowan-veiled
by early autumn,
stubblephantom,
cabbage-whites in your breath,
let the hands of many clocks revolve,
clamor with vesper bells,
gong
the golden persistent hour
that so firmly continues to tan,
into a trembling heart!

You:—world of difference!
Only gods rest thus
or the robes
of untoppleable Titans,
long-created,
embroidered so deeply
the butterflies and flowers
into their orbits!

Or a slumber of pristine kind,
when no awakening was,
only golden warmth and purple berries,
nibbled by swallows, eternal ones,
that never fly away—
This note strike, gong
this hour,
for
when you fall silent,
downward the forest-edges press,
thick with poplars, already cooler.

—Translated from the German by Christopher Middleton

(from *Statische Gedichte*, 1948)

Lucian Blaga   [Romania]
1895–1961

Born in Lancrăm, Transylvania into the family of a
Romanian Orthodox priest, Lucian Blaga was edu-
cated in German with a philosophical focus, includ-
ing the teachings of Lessing, Nietzsche and Bergson.
After graduating from the seminary, Blaga attended
the University of Vienna, studying philosophy and
biology.

Lucien Blaga

A year later, in 1919, he published his first collec-
tion of poetry, *Poemele luminii (Poems of Light)*, and
soon became one of the founders of the journal
Gîndirea, which was to become one of the most in-
novative magazines in Romania before the War. Two
years later he published another collection, *Pasii
profetului* (In the Footsteps of the Prophet), followed
by dramas and, in 1924, another collection of po-
etry, *În marea trecere* (In the Great Passage).

During this same period Blaga began his distinguised career as a journalist and diplomat,
serving as press attaché in Vienna beginning in 1932 and later as ambassador to Portugal. In 1939
he returned to Romania to become professor of philosophy at the University of Cluj. During
this period he became a member of the Romanian Academy and wrote important philosophi-
cal writings that would later make up the *Trilogia culturii*, which, along with *Trilogia cunoașterii*
and *Trilogia valorilor*, outlined methods for exploring what he described as "ultimate reality"
and a new cultural theory in which he tied culture to the expression of a metaphysics. Late in
the 1930s and early 1940s Blaga published his last two collections of poetry, including *La curțile
dorului (At the Court of Yearning)* and *Nebănuitele trepte*.

BOOKS OF POETRY

Poemele luminii (1919); *Pasii profetului* (1921); *În marea trecere* (1924); *Lauda somnului* (1929);
La cumpăna apelor (1933); *La curțile dorului* (1938); *Nebănuitele trepte* (1943); *Opere* [5 volumes]
(1974–1977).

ENGLISH LANGUAGE TRANSLATIONS

Poems of Light, translated by Roy MacGregor-Hastie, Don Eulert, Stefan Avadanei and Mikhail
Borgdan (Bucharest: Minerva, 1975); *Poezii/Poems*, edited by Michael Taub and translated by
Alfred Margul-Sperber (Bucharest: Minerva, 1981/Chapel Hill: Department of Romance Lan-
guages, University of North Carolina, 1983); *At the Court of Yearning*, translated and introduced
by Andrei Codrescu (Columbus: Ohio State University Press/A Sandstone Book, 1989).

A Man Bends over the Edge

I bend over the edge:
is it the sea
or my poor thought?

My soul falls deeply
slipping like a ring
from a finger weakened by fever.
Come, end, sprinkle ash on things.
There is no longer a path.
No longer am I haunted by a call.
Come, end.

I raise myself slightly from the earth
on one elbow
to listen.
Water beats against a shore.
Nothing else, nothing,
nothing.

—Translated from the Romanian by Andrei Codrescu

(from *În marea trecere*, 1924)

Heraclitus by the Lake

The paths come together by the green waters.
Silences crowd here, inhuman and abandoned.
Hush, dog, sniffing the wind with your nose!
Don't chase away the memories that come
to bury themselves, crying in their own ashes.

Leaning on a tree stump I try to guess my fate
from the palm of an autumn leaf.
Time, which way do you go
when you take a shortcut?

My steps echo in shadow
like rotten fruit
falling from an unseen tree.
O the stream's voice is sore with age!

Each movement of the hand
is one more doubt.
Sorrows call in the secret
ground below.

I throw thorns into the lake:
I am undone in the ripples.

—*Translated from the Romanian by Andrei Codrescu*

(from *În marea trecere*, 1924)

The Magic Bird
Molded in gold by C. Brâncuși

High-signed Orion blesses you
in the sudden wind.
A tear shedding above you
its high and holy geometry.

You lived once on a sea bottom
and circled closely the solar fire.
Your cry sounded from floating forests
over the first waters.

Are you a bird? A traveling bell?
Or a creature, an earless jug perhaps?
A golden song spinning
above our fear of dead riddles?

Living in the dark of tales
you play ghostly reed pipes
to those who drink sleep
from black subterranean poppies.

The light in your green eyes is
phosphorus peeled from old bones.
Listening to wordless revelation
you are lost in flight in celestial grass.

You guess profound mysteries
under the hewn domes of your afternoons.
Soar on endlessly
but do not reveal to us what you see.

—Translated from the Romanian by Andrei Codrescu

(from *Lauda somnului*, 1929)

Old City

Night. The hours turn
without urging.
Be still—clock hands
stop—sighing
on the ultimate sign.

Creatures of sleep
crawl under gates—
red dogs and trouble.
On the streets—tall and thin
the rain walks on stilts.

Old weary wind between walls
shakes dirt and iron gates.
Countrymen from bygone times
flash up a moment and vanish.

The black tower stands its ground
counting the years of defeat.
Be still—the stone saint
just extinguished his halo.

—Translated from the Romanian by Andrei Codrescu

(from *Lauda somnului*, 1929)

Enchanted Mountain

I enter the mountain: a stone gate quietly shuts.
Dream and bridge fly me up.
What violet lakes! What vital time!
The gold fox barks from the ferns.

Holy beasts lick my hands: strange,
under a spell, they stalk with eyes turned within.
Buzzing through the sleep of crystals
the bees of death fly. And the years. The years.

—Translated from the Romanian by Andrei Codrescu

(from *La cumpăna apelor*, 1933)

Divine Touch

What apparition! Ah, what light!
A white star fell into the garden,

Unexpected, unsought. Luck,
arrow, flower, fire.

In the high grass, in the wide silk,
it fell from the house of time.

A star came back to our world.
My hands bear its scar.

—Translated from the Romanian by Andrei Codrescu

(from *La cumpăna apelor*, 1933)

At the Court of Yearning

Our vigils: flour sifters.
Time passes through—
white dust in our hair.
Rainbows catch fire still:
we wait. We await

the solitary hour
to share in the green
kingdom, the sunlit heaven.

We are still:
wooden spoons forgotten
in the gruel of long days.

We are the guests on the porch
of the new light
at the court of yearning,
neighbors of the sky.

We wait to catch a glimpse
through gold columns
of the age of fire—
our daughters come out
to crown the doorways with laurel.

Now and then a tear springs up
to bury itself painlessly in the cheek—
who knows what pallid star it feeds?

—*Translated from the Romanian by Andrei Codrescu*

(from *La curţile dorului*, 1938)

Awakening

The tree starts. March echoes.
The bees gather and mix in their combs
awakening, honey, and wax.

Unsure between two borders,
its veins reaching under seven fields,
my tree, my chosen one, sleeps,
dragon of the horizon.

My tree.
The wind shakes it, March echoes.
The powers join together
to relieve it of the weight of its being,
to raise it from sleep, from its divine state.

From the height of the mountain
who sifts to cover it with so much light?

Like tears—the buds overwhelm it.
Sun, sun, why did you wake him?

—*Translated from the Romanian by Andrei Codrescu*

(from *La curţile dorului*, 1938)

Magic Sunrise

This is the way it was, the way it will be always.
I wait with my flower of flames in my hand.
Disturbing my greatly exaggerated weeks
the moon powerfully rises.

An earthquake shakes the midnight spheres.
In space—river, shadows, towers, hooves.
The hieratic star liturgically undresses the country.

Up there in the light how fragile the mountain!
The gods' cities crumble in the eyes of children
like old silk.
How holy matter is,
all sound to the ear!

—*Translated from the Romanian by Andrei Codrescu*

(from *Nebănuitele trepte*, 1943)

Jorge Carrera Andrade [Ecuador]
1903–1978

Jorge Carrera Andrade was born in Quito, Ecuador, the son of a liberal-minded judge. In the atmosphere of his home, Carrera Andrade quickly became aware of the social injustices of his countrymen, particularly those of the Ecuadorian Incas. This was much of the subject matter of his early poetry, and would remain with him as he traveled internationally, becoming Eucador's representative to UNESCO.

He began his literary career in his early teens, editing the magazine *La idea*. His first books, published in 1922 and 1926, were *Estanque inefable* and *La guirnalda del silencio*. In 1928, he traveled abroad, studying in France, Germany, and Spain. Throughout the 1930s, he remained in France, where he served as editor of the publishing house, Cuadernos del Hombre Nuevo. Beginning in 1940 he served, for several years, as the Ecuadorian consul to San Francisco.

Carrera Andrade's poetry is not experimental nor hermetic, but known for its lucid qualities and for its highly structured forms. "True poetry," as he writes, "is only that which has fallen from combat with the angel." However, his social concerns and the metaphors drawn from his own culture, particularly those of *El hombre planetario* (1959, The Planetary Man), lend a deep richness of imagery and feeling to his work.

BOOKS OF POETRY:

Estanque Inefable (Quito, 1922); *La guirnalda del silencio* (Quito: Imprenta Nacional, 1926); *Boletines de mar y tierra* (Barcelona: Cevantes, 1930); *El tiempo manual* (Madrid: Ediciones Literatura, 1935); *Rol de la manzana: Poesías (1926-1929)* (Madrid: Espasa-Calpe); *La hora de las ventanas iluminadas* (Santiago de Chile: Ercilla, 1937); *Biografía para uso de lo pájaros* (Paris: Cuadernos del Hombre Nuevo, 1937); *Registro del mundo* (Quito: Universidad Central, 1940); *País secreto* (Tokyo: published by the author, 1940); *Canto al Puente de Oakland/To the Bay Bridge* (San Francisco: Hoover Library on War / Stanford University, 1941); *Lugar de origen* Caracas: Editiones Suma, 1944); *Poesís escogidas* (Caracas: Editiones Suma, 1945); *Registro del mundo, antologia poetica. 1922-1939* (México: Seneca, 1945); *Canto a las fortalezas volantes: Cuaderno del paracaidista* (Caracas: Ediciones Destino, 1945); *Edades poeticas, 1922-1956* (Quito: Casa de la Cultura Ecuatoriana, 1958); *Mi vida en poemas: Ensayo autocritico seguido de una seleccion poetica* (Caracas: Ediciones Casa del Escritor, 1962); *Hombre planetario* (Quito: Casa de la Cultura Ecuatoriana, 1963); *Obra poetica completa* (Quito: Casa de la Cultura Ecuatoriana, 1976).

ENGLISH LANGUAGE TRANSLATIONS:

Secret Country: Poems, translated by Muna Lee (New York: Macmillan, 1946); *Visitor of Mist,* trans. by G. R. Coulthard (London: Williams & Norgate, 1950); *Selected Poems of Jorge Carrera Andrade*, translated by H. R. Hays (Albany: State University of New York Press, 1972).

The Clock
For Jaime Torres Bodet

Clock:
time's stonecutter.

The pendulum pounds at the hardest wall,
stubborn chisel of night.

The vanilla plant, awakened
composes suites of smell throughout the closets.

Watching over the clock,
in hushed slippers, silence stalks.

—Translated from the Spanish by Douglas Messerli

(from *La guirnalda del silencia*, 1926)

Spring and Company

The almond tree buys a dress
To take its first communion. The sparrows
Announce their green merchandise in doorways.
April has already sold
All of its white goods, its January masks,
And today is only concerned with puffing
Propaganda into every corner.

Rushes made of glass. Overturned bottles of perfume.
Rugs for schoolchildren to walk on.
Little baskets. Batons
Of cherries. Oversize gloves on
The ducks in the pond. Stork: a flying parasol.

Typewriter of breeze in the leaves,
Fragrant inventory.
Turn to the showcase of the night:
Cross of diamonds, little red lanterns
And rosary of precious stones.

March has lit sparks in the grass

And the useless old spruce tree has put on green spectacles.
After several months spring will have ready
An order of jars of preserved fruit,
Grapes—glands of sweet crystal—
And gilded leaves in which to pack sadness.

—Translated from the Spanish by H. R. Hays

(from *La guirnalda del silencia*, 1926)

Dining Room Mirror
To Alfonso Reyes

The dining room mirror
Builds
With squares and figures
Of snowy geometry.

It hoists palpitant planes
Toward its blue level.
It takes the measure of objects
With its compasses of light.

It shuffles certainties.
It fences with diameters.
It lines up lights.

The naked water bottle
Breaks its crystal ruler
And a slanting stream of diamonds
Issues toward the dark table.

Objects propel,
Along wires of air,
Their telegraphy of reflections.

The colors burst.
Light from the gay bevels
Strikes the eyelashes.

Vertical pools
With diagonals of ice.

Twins with the real,
The virginal breasts of the fruit bowl.

World, animated
With a glittering consciousness.
Trigonometry of light.
Visual ideas.

Life cut into patterns:
The saltcellar is wisdom;
The oysters, memory.

The pear is sculpture
In molds of air;
The coffee, intelligence,
And the sugar bowl, an angel.

—Translated from the Spanish by H. R. Hays

(from *Boletines de mar y tierra*, 1930)

Traveler's Bulletin

Over the tiled roof of the world
The cock hung out his bright colored chant to dry.
The light was by then as heavy as a fruit.

The country offered me tablets of the law.
The plow was made of the ancient wood
of the cross.

The latitude of the equator was
A ring of pain
On the finger of the heart.

In a ship with twenty funnels
I launched my baggage of parrots
Toward the other end of the world.

The alphabet of the constellations blazed.
Like children the ports whirled gaily
On the carousel of the horizon.

The seas and the four winds
Mutinied
Against my admiral dreams.

Anchor: iron cloverleaf.
The captain plucked you from an ancient continent
I saw the towers laded with their sacks of clouds
And the derricks, storks
With baskets in their beaks.

Europe set mechanical plows
Going with the rhythm of oil.
Through its irridescent straw
The wheat sucked at the lime of the soil.

But all the joy of the world
As it rose through chimneys
Was converted into smoke.

On the blank page of flour
Mills were printing
The wheat's proletarian oratory.

Cities were speaking through the breadth of the air.
I discovered man. Then
I understood my message.

—*Translated from the Spanish by H. R. Hays*

(from *Boletines de mar y tierra*, 1930)

Sum

The windmill, the drum, and the rose,
the accordion, the water-pail, the scarecrow;
the chickencoop ladder, the sombrero without shade,
the wall where the sun sticks up his white posters.

The spade turning out identical volumes of earth
and the brilliant birds that ripen on the branches.
The air that lives its dream in glassware
and the walking stick hooked to the straw-bottomed chair.

Lettuce marching down to the river like schoolchildren,
radishes, Red Riding-hoods who live underground.
The watering-pot, the nest, the fungi on wood:
green ciphers, animated sums.

—Translated from the Spanish by Muna Lee

(from *El tiempo manual*, 1935)

Blaise Cendrars [Frédéric Sauser] [Switzerland]
1887–1961

Francis Picabia

Blaise Cendrars

Although little is known of his early life—which throughout his life Cendrars kept secret—it is known that he was born Frédéric Sauser in 1887 in La Chaux-de-Fonds, Switzerland. During his infancy he lived, perhaps, in Egypt and in his later childhood, more certainly, in Naples. After education in England and Paris, Sauser returned in 1907 to Switzerland as a student in Basel, moving perhaps to Leipzig, and then to Bern. By 1910, he found his way to Paris, where, with fellow student Féla Poznanska, he translated letters and documents. Among the artists he first met was Marc Chagall, but basically Sauser was a failure in the art and literary worlds. For lack of funds, Féla was forced to visit relatives in the United States, while Sauser traveled to Saint Petersburg. Working as a language teacher, he attempted to return to Paris, but was unable to find the money until Féla mailed him a boat ticket for New York.

Living for a while with Féla's relatives in the Bronx, Sauser met the opera singer, Enrico Caruso and visited Stieglitz's galleries at 291; but the New York stay only reconfirmed his need to return to Paris. To make ends meet, he played the piano in a Bowery movie house, while Féla taught at the Ferrar School, founded by anarchist Emma Goldman. In New York Sauser took on the name of Blaise Cendrars, returning to Paris via Switzerland.

Over the next two years, Cendrars was active in the great avant-garde scene of the day. He worked with Guillaume Apollinaire, had poems published in journals, and made close friends with Fernand Léger, Robert and Sonia Delaunay, the boxer Arthur Cravan, and others. His closest drinking companion was Modigliani. Cendrars was active during this period in exhibitions and readings from Saint Petersburg to Berlin. *Panama* and *Elastic Poems* were also written during these years; and a son, Odilon, was born to Féla and Cendrars in 1914. A few days later, Cendrars was on his way to join The Foreign Legion.

In 1915, assaulting the Navarin Farm, in Champagne, Cendrars lost his right arm, and returned to Paris. At first the city was culturally deserted, but gradually poets and artists returned, and Cendrars was again involved in poetry readings and concerts with Apollinaire, Max Jacob, Pierre Reverdy, Erik Satie, Darius Milhaud, Arthur Honegger, and others of the avant-garde.In 1917, however, he left Paris with Féla and his two sons for the small town of Méréville, where he wrote *The End of the World Filmed by the Angel of Notre-Dame* and other works. In the same year, Cendrars began to move apart from his wife, traveling to Cannes where he worked with Abel Gance, eventually serving as his assistant on *La Roue*. Later, with the help of Jean Cocteau, he became the artistic director of La Sirène editions, where he published contemporary authors alongside authors such as Lautréamont and de Gourmont.

From 1912 to 1924, Cendrars also traveled to South America five times, lecturing in Brazil and other countries. During these years he completed his poetic activity and turned to fiction, writing *Sutter's Gold* in 1925, *Moravagine* in 1926, and *Dan Yack* in 1929. During the 1930s, he continued writing, mostly as a journalist, reporting on Hollywood and popular figures such as O. Henry and Al Capone. At the end of the decade, however, he returned to writing fiction, first with *Histoires vraies* (*True Stories*), *La Main coupée* (*Lice*), *L'Homme foudroyé* (*The Astonished Man*), *Bourlinguer* (*Planus*), and *Le Lotissement du ciel*.

The late 1940s and 1950s were a time of revising and overseeing the collected publication of his works. In 1956 and 1958 he suffered paralyzing strokes. In the year of the second stroke, he was awarded the Légion d'Honneur. In 1961 he was awarded the Grand Prix Littéraire de Paris. On January 21, 1961, Cendrars died.

BOOKS OF POETRY:

Les Pâques (Easter in New York) (Paris: Édition des Hommes Nouveaux); *La Prose du Transsibérien et de la Petite Jeanne de France (The Prose of the Trans-Siberian and of Little Jeanne of France)* (Paris: Édition des Hommes Nouveaux, 1913); *Séquences (Sequences)* (Paris: Édition des Hommes Nouveaux, 1913); *La Guerre au Luxembourg (The War in Luxembourg)* (Paris: Niestlé, 1916); *Le Panama ou les Aventures de mes sept oncles (Panama, or the Adventures of My Seven Uncles)* (Paris: Éditions de la Sirène, 1918); *Du Monde Entier (Les Pâques à New York; Prose du Transsibérien; Panama)* (Paris: Éditions de la Nouvelle Revue Française, 1919); *Dix-neuf poèmes élastiques (Nineteen Elastic Poems)* (Paris: Au Sans Pareil, 1919); *Kodak (Documentaires) (Kodak [Documentary])* (Paris: Stock, Dellamain, Boutelleau, 1924); *Le Formose* (Part I of *Feuilles de route*) (Paris: Au Sans Pareil, 1924); *Poésies complètes de Blaise Cendrars* (Paris: Denoël, 1944); *Oeuvres complètes de Blaise Cendrars* (8 vols.) (Paris: Denoël, 1960–1965; *Oeuvres complètes de Blaise Cendrars* (15 vols) (Paris: Denoël, 1968–1971).

ENGLISH LANGUAGE TRANSLATIONS:

Panama or the Adventures of My Seven Uncles, translated by John Dos Passos (New York and London: Harper & Brothers, 1931) [includes *The Trans-Siberian, Panama* and selections from *Kodak* and *Feuilles de route*); *Selected Writings of Blaise Cendrars*, edited with a Critical Intoduction by Walter Albert, translated by Walter Albert, John Dos Passos and Scott Bates (New York: New Directions, 1966); *Complete Postcards from the Americas*, translated by Monique Chefdor (Berkeley: University of California Press, 1976) [includes *Documentaires, Feuilles de route* and *Sud-Américaines*]; *Selected Poems*, translated by Peter Hoida, with an Introduction by Mary Ann Caws (Harmondsworth, England: Penguin, 1979); *Complete Poems*, translated by Ron Padgett, with an Introduction by Jay Bochner (Berkeley: University of California Press, 1992).

OpOetic

to Jean COctO

what crimes are
not cOmmitted
in   thy   name!

Once upon a time there were pOets who spOke with rOund mOuths
Round as salami her beautiful eyes and smOke
Ophelia's hair Or the lyre Orpheus strOked
You belch up rOund hats to find a strOke-of-genius rhyme sharp as
 teeth that would nibble your lines
Open-mouthed
Since you like smOke rings why don't you repeat *smOke*
It's too easy or too hard
The 7 pawns and the Queens are there as commas
Oh POEtry
Ah! Oh!
COcOa
Since you like cowboys why don't you write *cowpOke*
It's a written grOan that'll make the French crOak
The English clOwn did it with his legs
The way AretinO made love
The Mind envies the circus poster and the alphabetical pOsitions of the Snake Man
Where are the pOets who spOke with rOund mOuths?

We have to loosen up their b **O** nes
z enfant
h

POETRY

Nov. '16

—*Translated from the French by Ron Padgett*

(originally published in 1917, reprinted in the magazine *L'Oeuf dur*, 1923)

Homage to Guillaume Apollinaire

The bread is rising
France
Paris
An entire generation
I address the poets who were there
Friends
Apollinaire is not dead
You followed an empty hearse
Apollinaire is a magus
He's the one who was smiling in the silk of the flags at the windows
He enjoyed throwing you flowers and wreaths
While you walked behind his hearse
Then he bought a little three-colored cockade
I saw him that same night demonstrating on the boulevards
He was astride the hood of an American truck and waving an enormous
    international flag spread out like an airplane
LONG LIVE FRANCE

The times change
The years roll by like clouds
The soldiers have gone back home
To the houses
Where they live
And look a new generation is rising
The dream of the BREASTS is coming true!
Little French children, half English, half black, half Russian, a bit
    Belgian, Italian, Annamite, Czech
One with a Canadian accent, another with Hindu eyes
Teeth face bones joints lines smile bearing
They all have something foreign about them and are still part of us
Among them, Apollinaire, like that statue of the Nile, the father of the
    waters, stretched out with kids that flow all over him
Between his feet, under his arms, in his beard
They look like their father and go their own way
And they all speak the language of Apollinaire

Paris, November 1918

—*Translated from the French by Ron Padgett*

from *Nineteen Elastic Poems*

2. *Tower*

1910
Castellammare
I was dining on an orange in the shade of an orange tree
When suddenly . . .
It wasn't the eruption of Vesuvius
It wasn't the cloud of grasshoppers, one of the ten plagues of Egypt
Nor Pompeii
It wasn't the resuscitated cries of giant mastodons
It wasn't the heralded Trumpet
Nor Pierre Brisset's frog
When, suddenly,
Fires
Jolts
Surging
Spark of simultaneous horizons
My sex

          O Eiffel Tower!
I didn't give you golden slippers
I didn't make you dance on crystal tiles
I didn't vow you to the Python like a Carthaginian virgin
I didn't clothe you in the peplos of Greece
I never made you wander about in a circle of menhirs
I didn't name you Rood of David or Wood of the Cross
Lignum Crucis

          O Eiffel Tower
Giant fireworks of the Universal Exposition!
Over the Ganges
At Benares
Among the onanistic spinning tops of Hindu temples
And the colored cries of the multitudes of the East
You lean, graceful Palm Tree!
It was you who in the legendary era of the Hebrews
Confounded men's tongues
O Babel!
And a few thousand years later, it was you who fell again in tongues of
    fire onto the Apostles gathered in your church
On the open sea you're a mast
And at the North Pole

You shine with all the magnificence of the aurora borealis with your
    radio waves
The lianas grow through and around the eucalyptus
And you are floating, old trunk, on the Mississippi
When
Your mouth opens
And a cayman grabs a black man's thigh
In Europe you're like a gallows
(I'd like to be the tower, to hang from the Eiffel Tower!)
And when the sun goes down behind you
Bonnot's head rolls beneath the guillotine
In the heart of Africa it's you running
Giraffe
Ostrich
Boa
Equator
Monsoons
In Australia you've always been taboo
You're the gaff hook Captain Cook used to steer his boat of adventurers
O celestial plummet!
For the Simultaneous Delaunay, to whom I dedicate this poem,
You're the brush he dips in light

Gong tom-tom Zanzibar jungle animal X rays express scalpel symphony
You are everything
Tower
Ancient god
Modern animal
Solar spectrum
Subject of my poem
Tower
World tour tower
Moving tower

      August 1913

   —Translated from the French by Ron Padgett

(from *Dix-neuf poèmes élastiques*, 1919)

11. Bombay Express

The life I've led
Keeps me from suicide
Everything leaps
Women roll beneath the wheels
Screaming
The jalopies are fanned out at the station entrances.
I have music under my fingernails.

I never have liked Mascagni
Nor art nor Artists
Nor barriers nor bridges
Nor trombones nor trumpets
I don't know anything anymore
I don't understand anymore. . .
Such a caress
That the map is trembling from it

This year or next year
Art criticism is as idiotic as Esperanto
Brindisi
Good-bye good-bye

I was born in that town
And my son too
He whose forehead is like his mother's vagina

   —Translated from the French by Ron Padgett

(from *Dix-neuf poèmes élastiques*, 1919)

from *Kodak* / "River"

Mississippi

    Right here the river's almost as wide as a lake
    The yellowish muddy water rolls between two marshy banks
    Aquatic plants extending the acreage of the cotton fields
    Here and there appear the towns and villages lurking back in some little
        bay with their factories with their tall black chimneys with their long
        piers on pilings running way out into the water

Overwhelming heat
The ship's bell rings for lunch
The passengers sport checked suits blinding ties sunset-red vests like
    flaming cocktails and Louisiana hot sauce

You see a lot of crocodiles
The young ones frisky and wriggling
The big ones their backs covered with greenish moss just drifting along

The luxuriant vegetation indicates the approach of the tropical zone
Gigantic bamboos palm trees tulip trees laurels cedars
The river itself is now twice as wide
Dotted with floating islands from which our boat scares up clouds of
    waterfowl
Steamboats sailboats barges boats of all kinds and enormous rafts
A yellow steam rises from the overheated river

Now there are hundreds of crocs thrashing around us
You hear the dry snapping of their jaws and you see very clearly their
    wild little eyes
The passengers get a kick out of firing into them with hunting rifles
When a sharpshooter kills or mortally wounds one
Its fellows rush to tear it
To pieces
With small cries rather like the wailing of a newborn baby

   —*Translated from the French by Ron Padgett*

(from *Kodak*, 1924 / from "River")

from *Kodak* / "The North"

I. Spring

The Canadian springtime is the most invigorating and powerful in the world
Beneath the thick blanket of snow and ice
Suddenly
Generous nature
Tufts of violets pink white and blue
Orchids sunflowers tiger lilies
Down the venerable avenues of maple black ash and birch
The birds fly and sing

In shrubs budding again with new and tender shoots
The happy sunlight is the color of anise

Woods and farmlands stretch away from the road for over five miles
It's one of the biggest pieces of property in Winnipeg
On it rises a solid stone farmhouse something like a manor house
This is where my good friend Coulon lives
Up before daybreak he rides from farm to farm on his big bay mare
The earflaps of his rabbitskin hat dangle on his shoulders
Dark eyes and bushy brows
Very chipper
Pipe on his chin

The night is foggy and cold
A hard west wind bends and sways the firs and larches
A small glow is spreading
An ember crackles
It smolders and then burns through the brush
Clumps of resinous trees thrash around in the wind
Wham wham huge torches burst
The fire moves along the horizon with a majestic slowness
Black trunks and white trunks turn blood red
A dome of chocolate smoke out of which a million burning bits and
    sparks are flying spinning upward and sideways
Behind this curtain of flame you can see massive shadows twisting and
    crashing to the ground
Resounding axes chopping
An acrid haze spreads over the incandescent forest which a gang of
    lumberjacks are circumscribing

II. Country

Magnificent landscape
Green forests of fir beech chesnut cut with ripe fields of wheat oats
    buckwheat hemp
Everything breathing abundance
And it's absolutely deserted
Every great once in a while you run into a farmer driving a cartload of fodder
In the distance the birches are like columns of silver

III. Hunting and Fishing

Wild duck pintail teal goose lapwing bustard
Grouse thrush
Arctic hare snow partridge ptarmigan
Salmon rainbow trout eel
Gigantic pike and crawfish that taste particularly exquisite

Carbine across the back
Bowie knife in the belt
The hunter and the redskin are bent beneath the weight of the game
Strings of wood doves red-legged partridge
Wild peacock
Wild turkey
And even a big reddish-brown and white eagle brought down from the clouds

IV. Harvest

A six-cylinder and two Fords out in the field
All around and as far as you can see the slightly tilted sheaves from a
    checkerboard of wavering rhomboids
Not a tree
From the north the chugging and clatter of the thresher and hay wagon
And from the south the twelve empty trains coming to load the wheat

—*Translated from the French by Ron Padgett*

(from *Kodak*, 1924 / "The North")

PERMISSIONS

"from *Nineteen Elastic Poems*," "OpOetic," "from *Kodak* / River," and "Homage to Guillaume Apollinaire"
Reprinted from *Complete Poems*, trans. by Ron Padgett, with an Introduction by Jay Bochner (Berkeley:
University of California Press, 1992). Copyright ©1992 by Ron Padgett. Reprinted by permission of the
University of California Press.

Forugh Farrokhzad [Iran]
1935–1967

One of the major women poets of the Arab world, Forugh Farrokhzad attended school in Tehran without finishing her diploma. At sixteen she was unhappily married, and was soon divorced, giving birth to a son, who remained the custody of her husband.

Writing poetry since the age of fourteen, Farrokhzad concentrated on her art, traveling to Italy, Germany, and England, which, in turn, highly influenced her work. She also turned to film-making, producing a a documentary for UNESCO in 1965.

Her first collection of poetry, *Asir* (The Captive) appeared in 1952, and she used that title also for her second collection of 1955. This second collection made her the topic of great scandal throughout Iran, since as a woman she wrote freely about sensuality

Drawing, self portrait of Forugh Farrokhzad

and love. Over the next several years she produced further volumes, *Divar* (The Wail) in 1956, *'Osyan* (The Rebellion) in 1968; and *Tavvalod-e degar* (Another Birth) in 1964. The last volume has been translated into English.

In 1967 Farrokhzad was killed in an automobile accident.

BOOKS OF POETRY

Asir (1952); *Asir* (1955); *Divar* (1956); *'Osyan* (1958); *Tavvalod-e degar* (1964)

ENGLISH LANGUAGE TRANSLATIONS

Bride of Acacias: Selected Poems of Forugh Farrokhzad, trans. by Jascha Kessler with Amin Banani, with an Introduction by Amin Banani and Afterword by Farzaneh Milani (Delmar, New York: Caravan Books, 1982); Selections in *Literature East & West*, Volume 24 (1987).

Conquest of the Garden

The crow which flew over our heads
and descended
into the disturbed thought of a vagabond cloud
and the sound of which traversed
the breadth of the horizon like a short spear
will carry news of us to the city.

Everyone knows, everyone knows
that you and I have seen the garden from that cold sullen window
and that we have plucked the apple
from that playful branch beyond reach.

Everyone is afraid everyone is afraid,
but you and I joined with lamp, water and mirror
and we are not afraid.

I am not talking about the flimsy linking of two names
and embracing in the old pages of a ledger.
I'm talking about my fortunate tresses
with the burnt anemone of your kiss
and the intimacy of our bodies,
and the glow of our nakedness like fish scales in the water.
I am talking about the silvery life of a song
which the small fountain sings at dawn.

We asked wild rabbits one night
in that green flowing forest
and the shells full of pearls
in that turbulent coldblooded sea
and the young eagles
on that strange overwhelming mountain
what should be done.

Everyone knows, everyone knows
we found our way into the cold and quiet dream of phoenixes.
We found truth in the garden
in the embarassed look of a nameless flower,
and we found immortality in an endless moment
when two suns stared at each other.

I am not talking about timorous whispering in the dark.
I am talking about daytime and open windows and fresh air
and a stove in which useless things burn
and land which is fertile with a different planting,
and birth and evolution and pride.
I am talking about our loving hands
which have built across nights
a bridge of the message of perfume and light and breeze.
Come to the meadow
to the grand meadow and call me,
from behind the breaths of silk-tasseled acacias
just as the deer calls its mate.

The curtains are full of a hidden rancor,
and innocent doves look to the ground
from their white tower height.

—*Translated from the Farsi by Michael Craig Hillmann*

Another Birth

My whole being is a dark chant
that perpetuating you
will carry you to the dawn
of eternal growths and blossomings
in this chant I sighed you, sighed
in this chant
I grafted you to the tree, to the water,
to the fire.

Life is perhaps
a long street through which
a woman holding a basket
passes very day
life is perhaps
a rope with which a man
hangs himself from a branch
Life is perhaps
a child returning home from school.

Life is perhaps lighting up a cigarette
in the narcotic repose between two love-makings
or the absent gaze of a passerby
with a meaningless smile and a good morning.

Life is perhaps that enclosed moment
when my gaze destroys itself in the pupil of your eyes
and it is in the feeling that I will put
into the Moon's perception and the Night's impression.

In a room as big as loneliness
my heart which is as big as love
looks at the simple pretexts of its happiness
at the beautiful decay of flowers in the vase
at the saplings you planted in our garden
and the song of canaries
which sing to the size of a window.

Ah...this is my lot
this is my lot
my lot is a sky that is taken away
at the drop of a curtain
my lot is going down a flight of disused stairs
to regain something amid putrefaction and nostalgia
my lot is a sad promenade in the garden of memories
and dying in the grief of a voice that tells me I love your hands.

I will plant my hands in the garden
I will grow
I know I know I know
and swallows will lay eggs
in the hollow of my ink-stained hands.

I shall wear twin cherries as earrings
and I shall put dahlia petals on my fingernails.

There is an alley where the boys who were in love with me
still loiter with the same unkempt hair, thin necks and bony legs
and think of the innocent smiles of a little girl
who was blown away by the wind one night.

There is an alley that my heart has stolen from the streets of my childhood.

The journey of a form along the line of time
and inseminating the line of time with the form
a form conscious of an image returning from a feast in the mirror.

And it is in this way that someone dies and someone lives on.

No fisherman shall ever find a pearl
in a small brook that empties into a pool.

I know a sad little fairy
who lives in an ocean
and ever so softly plays her heart into a magic flute
a sad little fairy
who dies with one kiss each night
and is reborn with one kiss each dawn.

—Translated from the Farsi by Karim Emami with Forugh Farrokhzad

It Is Only Sound That Remains

Why should I stop, why?
The birds have gone in search of the blue direction.
The horizon is vertical, vertical,
and movement fountain-like,
and at the limits of vision shining planets spin.
The earth in elevation reaches repetition,
and air wells change into tunnels of connection.
And day is a vastness
which does not fit into the narrow mind of newspaper worms.

Why should I stop?
The road passes through the capillaries of life.
The condition of the planting environment of the uterus-like moon
will kill the corrupt cells.
And in the chemical space after sunrise
there is only sound,
sound that will be dream to the particles of time.
Why should I stop?

What can a swamp be?
What can a swamp be
but the spawning ground of corrupt insects?

Swollen corpses scrawl the morgues' thoughts,
the unmanly one has hidden his lack of manliness in blackness,
and bugs...ah when bugs talk,
why should I stop?
Cooperation of dead letters is futile,
and cannot rescue miserable thoughts.

I am a descendant of trees.
Breathing stale air depresses me.
A bird which had died advised me
to commit flight to memory.
The ultimate extent of all powers is union,
joining with the bright principle of the sun
and pouring into the consciousness of light.

It is natural for windmills to fall apart.

Why should I stop?
I clasp to my breast
the unripe bunches of wheat
and breastfeed them.

Sound, sound, only sound,
the sound of the limpid wish of water to flow,
the sound of the falling of starlight
on the layer of earth's femininity,
the sound of the binding of meaning's sperm
and the expansion of the shared mind of love.
Sound, sound, sound, only sound remains.

In the land of dwarfs,
the criteria of comparison have always traveled
in the orbit of zero.
Why should I stop?
I obey the four elements
and the job of drawing up the constitution of my heart
is not the business
of the local government of the blind.

What is the lengthy wild whimpering
in animals' sexual organs to me?
What to me
is the worm's humble movement

in the fleshy vacuum?
The bleeding ancestry of flowers
has commited me to life.
Are you familiar with the bleeding ancestry of the flowers?

—*Translated from the Farsi by Michael Craig Hillmann*

(1966)

from Let Us Believe in the Beginning of the Cold Season

And this is I
a woman alone
at the threshold of a cold season
at the beginning of understanding
the polluted existence of the earth
and the simple and sad pessimism of the sky
and the incapacity of these stone hands.

I am cold
I am cold and it feels like
I will never be warm again.

I shall give up lines
I shall give up counting, too.
And I shall seek refuge
from finite geometric figures
in sensuous dreams of vastitude.
I am naked, naked, naked
I am naked as the silence between words of love
all my wounds come from love
from love, love, love.
I have steered this wandering island
through the revolutions of the ocean
and the explosion of the mountain.
Breaking apart
is the secret of the whole of existence
from whose smallest particles the sun was born.

Let us believe
let us believe in the cold season
let us believe in the ruins of orchards of imagination
in abandoned sickles
and imprisoned seeds.
Look! What a heavy snow is falling...

—*Translated from the Farsi by Gita Tabatabai*

Pedro García Cabrera   [Canary Islands]
1905–1981

Born in Vallehermoso, La Gomera, Pedro García
Cabrera stayed for some of childhood in his father's
home in Seville before returning the Canaries, where
he lived until his death in 1981.

Pedro García Cabrera

After secondary school, García Cabrera began
writing for the *Gaceta de Tenerife*, later joining the
staff of the magazine *Hespérides*. His first book of
poetry, *Líquenes* (Lichens) appeared in 1928. A few
years later he helped to found the important maga-
zine of the Canarian indigenist movement, *Cartones*.
And from 1932–1936, he was a founder of the *Gaceta
de Arte*, representative of one of the brilliant cultural
movements of the Islands. To *Gaceta* he contributed
poems and essays, and in 1934 the journal pub-
lished his *Transparencias fugadas* (Fled Transparen-
cies), one of the major documents of literary surrealism of the Canary Islands.

When the Spanish Civil War broke out, García Cabrera was arrested for his socialist ideas
and deported to Villa Cisneros, from where he escaped. But upon the end of the War in 1936, he
was again arrested and imprisoned until 1946, whereupon he returned to Tenerife to work as a
diplomat. During these many years, he wrote numerous collections of poetry, including *Dársena
con despertadores* (Dock with Alarm Clocks), *La rodilla en el agua* (The Knee in the Water), *Los
senos de tina* (The Breasts of Ink), *Entre la guerra y tú* (Between War and You), *Romancero
cautivo* (Captive Ballad Book), *La arena y la intimidad* (Sand and Intimacy), *Hombros de ausencia*
(Shoulders of Absence), and *Viaje al interior de tu voz* (Journey to the Interior of Your Voice)—
all of which remained unpublished until his *Obras completas* (Complete Works) of 1987.

He continued to produce many collections of poetry that established his reputation in the
Canaries, including *Vuelta a la isla* (1968, Return to the Island), *Entre cuatro paredes* (1968, Be-
tween Four Walls), *Hora punta del hombre* (1969, Rush Hour of Man), *Las islas en que vivo* (1971,
The Islands Where I Live), *Elegías muertas de hambre* (1975, Elegies Dying of Hunger), *Ojos que
no ven* (1977, Eyes That Do Not See), and *Hacia la libertad* (1978, Towards Freedom). Other
books, uncompleted at his death, appear in his *Obras completas*.

BOOKS OF POETRY:

Líquenes (Santa Cruz de Tenerife: Editorial Hespérides, 1928); *Transparencias fugadas* (1934);
Dársena con despertadores (Santa Cruz de Tenerife: Ed. Gaceta de Arte, 1934); *La rodilla en el
agua* (written 1934–1935; Santa Cruz de Tenerife: Ed. Benchomo, 1981); *Dársena con despertadores*
(1936, in *Papeles Invertidos* (Santa Cruz de Tenerife, 1980); *Día de alondras* (Sta. Cruz de Tenerife:
Goya Ediciones, 1951); *La esperanza me mantiene* (Madrid: Artes Gráficas Argés, 1959);*Vuelta a
la isla* (Sta. Cruz de tenerife: Caja de Ahorros de Tenerife, 1968);*Entre cuatro paredes* (Ed. Gaceta
Semanal de las Artes, 1968);*Hora punta del hombre* (Las Palmas de Gran Canaria: Ed. Domingo
Velázquez, 1970);*Las islas en que vivo* (Sta. Santa Cruz de Tenerife: Ed. Nuestro Art, 1971); *Elegías*

muertas de hambre (Madrid: Ed.Rialp, 1975);*Ojos que no ven* (Madrid: Taller Eds. JB, 1977);*Hacia la libertad* (Las Palmas-St. Cruz de Tenerife: Ediciones, 1978); *A la mar fuí por naranjas* [collected works] (Las Palmas de Gran Canaria: Edirca, 1979); *Obras completas*, ed by Sebastián de la Nuez with Rafael Fernández and Nilo Palenzuela (Ed. Consejería de Cultura y Deportes el Gobierno Autónomo de Canarias, 1987).

ENGLISH LANGUAGE TRANSLATIONS:

Selections in *Contemporary Poetry from the Canary Islands*, translated by Louis Bourne, selected and introduced by Sebastián de la Nuez Caballero (London and Boston: Forest Books, 1992).

[With a compass of rainbow...]

With a compass of rainbow
They traced the horizon.
Center is the island:
Seaweed choked
By the blue fetter
That cut the feet of the roads.

The dense curtains
Have their backs turned to the little boats
Poking blues and scratching stained-glass windows.
The gaoler with infinite keys
Locked them in the cellars of heaven.

And not even in the calash of the breeze
Is there a spare space in the flight.

—*Translated from the Spanish by Louis Bourne*

(from *Líquenes*, 1928)

The bird of dreams speaks

Just as ghosts are not known for their habits,
I want to explain the key to my best acts.
So you will learn
That
To psychoanalyze the flight of butterflies
There is no better device than the magnets of my beak.
That I feel no envy for fog
For I myself am the true fog, adapted
To the shape of my globetrotting desires.
The fog you see in the field is just a mirage
That cannot endure the spiders of reflections.
That an insect, using the insomnias of my long
Lace tail, can darken the night of someone's temples.
What you will never know is if the roads
Face towards or away from passers-by
For it depends
On which of my wings points to the west of a cry.
No one will be able to understand that my greatest surprise

May be to find a fair-haired violin
On a greedy plain of ice,
Though he may know that the color of anxieties
Is that of weeping for a love ripened among nettles.
The same for a snail as for a sigh as for a hoof,
I would make a microphone
To hear the gasping of water in the light's depths.
If my death existed,
I would send for it to be found deep in my eyes
With the first top hat that passed by
Dressed in burning feathers.
There's just one word that inspires my tenderness,
That one balanced
On the tip of a rhetorician's tongue.
For me it never rains, but if it did,
They would be Gothic letters and cottons in flames.
This is my alcohol. Sip it while you sleep.
This time only I am going to lead you
To the angriest landscape on earth,
Bleeding to the right of a fantasy of larks.
No hope
Blinds me,
Both because I am at once all blindnesses
And because I slope down beyond every sea.

—*Translated from the Spanish by Louis Bourne*

(from *Dársena con despertadores* [1936] in *Papeles Invertidos,* 1980)

The open engagement

To the right of the voice of the statue's dream
A river of birds flows by.
The river is a little girl and the bird a key.
And the key a field of wheat
That opens a slow snail of a hundred days.
This means the hills of broken men
Are made of cardboard, wood and green walnuts.
But don't touch that anguish; it's all from the Sunday
When they created the nests in which tomorrow the
    adulterous stones will brood.
It's from that fish looking through the sea's eye

At how war is the tenderness guarding the empty beds
And peace that blood with which feet spatter their chains.
Let's go now. Don't pierce the shadow I had four years ago,
For my fingers ache with hunger and my heart with rains.
Better for you to sleep, to go on walking.
I'll wait for you till the tigers, on the lake shore, after the
    wine harvest,
Lying farmhands to the fields
And shoulders of someone on the deserted promises
    without water.

—Translated from the Spanish by Louis Bourne

(from *Entre la guerra y tú [1936–'39]* in *Obras completas 1*, 1987)

The lark of good fortune

Give me your green hand, seaweed,
Foam's faithful beloved,
For in it I want to read
The sea's good fortune,
That you are in love
None has any doubt:
Neither the beaches, nor the islands,
Nor the eyes of the rain.
Nor the rings, either,
Of wakes surrounding you,
Nor the breeze's does
Racing over the dunes.
Anxieties' blue vein
Beats in your ripe temples.
The salt is always weaving
Orange blossom for your wedding,
The sky, branches of stars,
The moon, ermine furs.
And the fish can no longer
Swim your deep waters
Without feeling they are nightingales
Of the caverns underwater.
And further down, in your
Liquid shadows' depths,
An instinct of corals

Dreams naked throats.
The birds of your domains
Fly you feather beds;
To you forest birds will bring
Epithalamiums of fruits.
(Here the green good fortune
Of seaweed is cut short.
But I can add—
Without boasting or bitterness—
That if the sea fell in love
More than he had ever done,
It was because my sweet friend
Wet her feet in the foam.)

—Translated from the Spanish by Louis Bourne

(from *Día de alondras*, 1951)

Tacoronte

To Ernesto Castro Fariñas

In this village
The schoolboys draw
Sluggish landscapes of shadow
With greys dying of grief.
The pomp of colors
Here amounts to nothing.
Neither the sunflower of afternoon
In the skies, nor the slope
Of greens uphill,
Nor even the blue lure
Of a rainy foot on the sea
Appear on their palates.
For the man of these fields
Feels his piece of earth
So deep inside himself,
In his closest intimacy,
That when at day's end
He sees his job fulfilled,
The evening grey is already
Ashes of the bonfire
That blazed, while he worked

Without lifting his head.
The sunset's idle show
Neither makes the grass sprout,
Nor satisfies hunger and thirst,
Nor redeems and frees him.
He devotes himself to his hands,
Hands with which he suddenly
Sows, in the same furrow,
His freedom and his censure.
He shares, from the last
Thirsty melancholies,
The equality of seeds
In the bosom of the earth
And that round darkness
Of the womb of harvets
Taking him back to the silence
Of maternal entrails.
Silence of Tacoronte
Hard as stone.
When you move away from
The highway's easy river,
This silence follows you
Like a bulldog
And against him there's no use
Shutting windows and doors.
Wherever you go,
His tongue keeps licking you.
This silence is the must
Fermented by wine-cellars,
The mirror in which rebellions
And sorrows see themselves.
It is the loneliness
Painted by the schoolboys;
It is the heart of man,
His veins pulsing rage;
Alone with ideas inside,
Lonelier, ideas outside.
Silence that never doubts
Treads firmly and tests
What still remains in us
Of island and volcano.
And amidst this silence
That yields to no one,
The night of Tacorante,

Vintageress of stars,
Into the comfort of her
Dark tresses, lets sink
The hands of him who works
And the brow of one who dreams.

—Translated from the Spanish by Louis Bourne

(from *Vuelta a la Isla*, 1968)

The broom

To my cousin, Rogelio Trujillo Cabrera, and Isabelita

She starts the day,
Greeting the mosaics one by one,
Stirring them in their calling as mirrors.
What joy to scatter so much night,
To erase so many rings under eyes,
To make the shadows leave in flight!
What a job hers, setting in motion
The linked activity of the things we love,
And they have almost managed to become us,
Lend us features, even a name,
The labored name of our preferences,
Earned with bare hands from years,
Building a face of surprises
With the flow of each instant,
The name we choose through that cosmos
Of habits and familiar belongings,
More real than the other given us by our parents.
And how a chore so floored
Can produce a dawn so difficult!
She preludes the orchestrated swarm
Of taps, the water's music,
The good days of oiled hinges,
Swaying her amazon breed
In passages, on patios and pavements,
Happy as a harp
Playing in the energy of two arms.
If only her press for purity could clean away
Stabbing ice, grim cries
And clouds of ash.

If she could at least take the dirt from our eyes
So we could see the linked light
Striking the walls outside and our foreheads.
The broom also feels misfortunes,
At times sweeping up tears
And the broken windowpanes of dreams,
And even genuine pieces of herself,
The useless feet of her hope,
Dead now the wish of walking by herself.
But without her Cindrella hustling,
The house could never get up,
Nor welcome friends,
Nor serve as a horse for the little ones.
For there is a great deal of grandmother
In the humanity of a broom.

—Translated from the Spanish by Louis Bourne

(from *Entre cuatro paredes*, 1968)

A bud from the sea...

To Justo Jorge Padrón

A bud from the sea has reached my feet.
Unexpectedly
It sprouted from the womb of a wave
With its body of sobbings and murmurs
As if it were truly a life.
Such pure vapor,
Such seething milk,
Crowned its hurried existence
So its spark of water left an opening
Not even to memory.
I have hardly been able to keep an instant
Its time of dying,
Its swift birth to death.
And maybe the whole soul of an island,
More than an obsession of rocks standing fast,
Is a bud of binding sea.

—Translated from the Spanish by Louis Bourne

(from *Las islas en que vivo*, 1971)

Hegemony of gadgets

Other forests came. New ways
Of wilting shadow desposed
Green lattices, the leaves foreboding
Coffered rhythms.
They condemned ears of grain to death.
The washing out of leafage was total
In valleys and mountains and plains.
Everything throbbed
By the kiss of a flower
Collapsed.
And earth filled up with scaffoldings
That were affected neither by springs
Nor senile autumns.
One single season,
In the chaos of spurrings, they imposed
Industrial centers.
Orchestras of metal symphonied
Clouds of smoke. Diagrams of sabbats
Maddened connecting rods and lightning bolts.
The lights kicked. They plunged us
Into the poverty of a sigh.

After so much crime,
Of murdering valid words
For the sake of plastics,
They found a clover
That had been saved from the fire.
The subjugated machines stopped,
Seeing the freedom of that marvel.
And the asphalt gave birth to green eyes,
Seeing the courage of a leaf.

—*Translated from the Spanish by Louis Bourne*

(from *Ojos que no ven*, 1977)

Permissions

"[With a compass of rainbow...]," "The bird of dreams speaks," "The open engagement," "The lark of good fortune," "Tacoronte," "The broom," "A bud from the sea...," and "Hegemony of gadgets,"
Reprinted from *Contemporary Poetry from the Canary Islands*, trans. by Louis Bourne; Selected and Introduced by Sebastián de la Nuez Caballero (London and Boston: Forest Books, 1992). Translations copyright ©1992 by Louis Bourne. Reprinted by permission of Louis Bourne.

Barbara Guest [USA]
1920

Barbara Guest

Born in North Carolina in 1920, Barbara Guest spent her childhood in Florida and California. After graduating from the University of California at Berkeley, she settled in New York City where she connected with the equally emerging New York Poets and artists of Abstract-Expressionism who were then to influence her poetry.

During the 1960s *The Location of Things, Poems,* and *The Blue Stairs* were published. *Moscow Mansions* (1973), *The Countess from Minneapolis* (1976), and in particular her novel *Seeking Air* (1978), pointed to a sense of structure moving in more varied and experimental directions. This was true of her acclaimed biography of the poet H.D., *Herself Defined* (1984), which had consumed five years, and especially of a major poem, *The Türler Losses* (1979), and of *Biography* (1980).

Fair Realism (1989) was followed by *Defensive Rapture* (1993), of which a critic has observed that Guest was now "pushing the reader into the spiritual and metaphysical possibilities of language itself." Both books were highly acclaimed: *Fair Realism* was awarded the Lawrence J. Lipton Prize for Poetry, and *Defensive Rapture* was chosen for the San Francisco State Poetry Award. At this same time, Guest left New York City, moving to Berkeley, California.

In 1995 her *Selected Poems* were published, and marked a continuing international recognition of her writing. The work was chosen as the best collection of new writing by the America Awards. Her *Quill, Solitary APPARITION* won the same award in 1996 for the best new book of poetry. In 1997 Guest took her work in yet newer directions with the publication of *The Confetti Trees*, fictional film scripts written in her highly lyrical style.

BOOKS OF POETRY

The Location of Things (New York: Tibor de Nagy, 1960); *Poems: The Location of Things; Archaics; The Open Skies* (Garden City, New York: Doubleday & Company, 1962); *The Blue Stairs* (New York: Corinth Books, 1968); *Moscow Mansions* (New York: Viking, 1973); *The Countess from Minneapolis* (Providence, Rhode Island: Burning Deck, 1976); *The Türler Losses* (Montréal: Mansfield Book Mart, 1979); *Biography* (Providence, Rhode Island: Burning Deck, 1980); *Quilts* (New York: Vehicle Editions, 1981); *Musicality* (Berkeley, California: Kelsey Street Press, 1988); *Fair Realism* (Los Angeles: Sun & Moon Press, 1989); *Defensive Rapture* (Los Angeles: Sun & Moon Press, 1993); *Stripped Tales* (Berkeley, California: Kelsey Street Press, 1995); *Selected Poems* (Los Angeles: Sun & Moon Press, 1995); *Quill, Solitary APPARITION* (Sausalito, California: The Post-Apollo Press, 1996); *The Confetti Trees* (Los Angeles: Sun & Moon Press, 1999); *If So, Tell Me* (London: Reality Street Editions, 1999).

Parachutes, My Love, Could Carry Us Higher

I just said I didn't know
And now you are holding me
In your arms,
How kind.
Parachutes, my love, could carry us higher.
Yet around the net I am floating
Pink and pale blue fish are caught in it,
They are beautiful,
But they are not good for eating.
Parachutes, my love, could carry us higher
Than this mid-air in which we tremble,
Having exercised our arms in swimming,
Now the suspension, you say,
Is exquisite. I do not know.
There is coral below the surface,
There is sand, and berries
Like pomegranates grow.
This wide net, I am treading water
Near it, bubbles are rising and salt
Drying on my lashes, yet I am no nearer
Air than water. I am closer to you
Than land and I am in a stranger ocean
Than I wished.

(from *Poems*, 1962)

Santa Fe Trail

I go separately
The sweet knees of oxen have pressed a path for me
ghosts with ingots have burned their bare hands
it is the dungaree darkness with China stitched
where the westerly winds
and the traveler's checks
the evensong of salesmen
the glistening paraphernalia of twin suitcases
where no one speaks English.
I go separately
It is the wind, the rubber wind
when we brush our teeth in the way station

a climate to beard. What forks these roads?
Who clammers o'er the twain?
What murmurs and rustles in the distance
in the white branches where the light is whipped
piercing at the crossing as into the dunes we simmer
and toss ourselves awhile the motor pants like a forest
where owls from their bandaged eyes send messages
to the Indian couple. Peaks have you heard?
I go separately
We have reached the arithmetics, are partially quenched
while it growls and hints in the lost trapper's voice
She is coming toward us like a session of pines
in the wild wooden air where rabbits are frozen,
O mother of lakes and glaciers, save us gamblers
whose wagon is perilously rapt.

(from *Poems*, 1962)

Red Lilies

Someone has remembered to dry the dishes;
they have taken the accident out of the stove.
Afterward lilies for supper; there
the lines in front of the window
are rubbed on the table of stone

The paper flies up
then down as the wind
repeats. repeats its birdsong.

Those arms under the pillow
the burrowing arms they cleave
as night as the tug kneads water
calling themselves branches

The tree is you
the blanket is what warms it
snow erupts from thistle;
the snow pours out of you.

A cold hand on the dishes
placing a saucer inside

her who undressed for supper
gliding that hair to the snow

The pilot light
went out on the stove

The paper folded like a napkin
other wings flew into the stone.

(from *Moscow Mansions,* 1973)

An Emphasis Falls on Reality

Cloud fields change into furniture
furniture metamorphizes into fields
an emphasis falls on reality.

"It snowed toward morning," a barcarole
the words stretched severely

silhouettes they arrived in trenchant cut
the face of lilies....

I was envious of fair realism.

I desired sunrise to revise itself
as apparition, majestic in evocativeness,
two fountains traced nearby on a lawn....

you recall treatments
of 'being' and 'nothingness'
illuminations apt
to appear from variable directions—
they are orderly as motors
floating on the waterway,

so silence is pictorial
when silence is real.

The wall is more real than shadow
or that letter composed of calligraphy
each vowel replaces a wall

a costume taken from space
donated by walls....

These metaphors may be apprehended after
they have brought their dogs and cats
born on roads near willows,

willows are not real trees
they entangle us in looseness,
the natural world spins in green.

A column chosen from distance
mounts into the sky while the font
is classical,

they will destroy the disturbed font
as it enters modernity and is rare....

The necessary idealizing of you reality
is part of the search, the journey
where two figures embrace

This house was drawn for them
it looks like a real house
perhaps they will move in today

into ephemeral dusk and
move out of that into night
selective night with trees,

The darkened copies of all trees.

(from *Fair Realism*, 1989)

Borrowed Mirror, Filmic Rise

Arriving speeds the chromatic
we stay with fire

arrows jasper pontifex declare
an imaginative risk.

fermented moss a
bulge in aramanth

motley filmic rise
that welds a natural

shield refreshed in hutch
of oak.

from borrowed mirror
rain a seized and

crystal pruner the limned
and eyed cowl

eyedusk.

commends internal habitude
bush the roof
day stare gliding
double measures.

qualms the weights of night
medusæ raft clothed sky
radiant strike the oars
skim cirrus.

evolve a fable husk
aged silkiness the roan
planet mowed like ears
beaded grip.

suppose the hooded grass
numb moat alum trench a solemn
glaze the sexual estuary
floats an edge.

(from *Defensive Rapture*, 1993)

The Minus Ones

She submitted a few stories she called *The Minus Ones*.

They came to her as short signals, as if they lived on her roof top. They rolled off the roof of her mouth climbed there from memory or from a table where empty cups glistened with tearfulness. Also menu-like out of her strung heart came surprising plots: Spanish women and high shoes, stories of valleys and boatless seas no cargoes. Rocks similar to the porpoises in her marine story appeared. They were made of coal hard yet they chipped flakes of coal dust blew off them soiling her clothes.

From her reading she borrowed a lake bottomless and a body without gravity flying over it. This appropriation brought on a serious malaise; she became plotless and her stories were bound without the usual wrapping of ribbon.

Seasons became important, ivy on green trees and the mournful rhododendron, icicles appeared more frequently. And meadows with horses. She neglected to include the rituals of contemporary life and the Scenario Department complained. When she wrote of wood burning she said the devils inside the fire were excited.

The fire scene destroyed any chance she had for her new stories to be accepted. They told her they liked real fires and not those of the imagination. Imagination was harmful and always messed up the set.

(from *The Confetti Trees*, 1999)

The Luminous

Patches of it

    on the lettuce a geography
    on trucks brilliant noise

      on the figure a disrobing
      radiance sweaters dumped

on water,

weightlifting there in the forest clump
striking at the underbrush, digging
past the clumsy curve

skipping certain passages, taking off
the sweater.

That fir cone found its voice on the path
in light after the sun came out

the postcard illuminates certain features in the face
the notebook lying on the windowsill,
the spindle back, the broken stem, all richer,

niceties tend to drop, also words like "many
loves" come forward the surprise of white stars

and the boots step by amazingly on the dried rich clay.

He swings his racket after it the luminous
the ball nearly swerves into it

those ancient people learning to count
surrounded by it, every day,

and navigators noting it there on the waves

the animus containing bits there on its subject
perched like sails,

bright rewards for preparing to strut forth
like the diver there on the board forced
by his greed into it.

Many loves changes to many times falling into
the day's lucid marshes

a tap on the shoulder or a first grasping that
object full of sparks

the wilderness untangled by it.

The fierceness with which it forged its memory,
its daylight, its absence.

Yes to the point of damages,
yes to the stunning infrequency,
yes to encourage with repetition its repetion,
yes to sober knowledge of its parsimony.

A few fir cones, sails, the stain removed,
blazes from the paper without lifting your hands.

(from *If So, Tell Me*, 1999)

PERMISSIONS

"Parachutes, My Love, Could Carry Us Higher," "Santa Fe Trail," "Red Lilies," and "An Emphasis Falls on Reality"
Reprinted from *Selected Poems* (Los Angeles: Sun & Moon Press, 1995). Copyright ©1995 by Barbara Guest. Reprinted by permission of Sun & Moon Press.

"Borrowed Mirror, Filmic Rise"
Reprinted from *Defensive Rapture* (Los Angeles: Sun & Moon Press, 1993). Copyright ©1993 by Barbara Guest. Reprinted by permission of Sun & Moon Press.

"The Minus Ones"
Reprinted from *The Confetti Trees* (Los Angeles: Sun & Moon Press, 1999). Copyright ©1999 by Barbara Guest. Reprinted by permission of Sun & Moon Press.

"The Luminous"
Reprinted from *If So, Tell Me* (London: Reality Street Editions, 1999). Copyright ©1999 by Barbara Guest. Reprinted by permission of Reality Street Editions.

Nikolai Gumilev [Russia]
1886–1921

The son of a navy doctor, Nikolai Gumilev was born in Kronstadt, Russia in (under the old calendar) 1886. He published his first poem while still in secondary school, and graduated from the school in Tsarskoe Selo in 1903.

Nikolai Gumilev

Two years later, while studying at the University of Petersburg, he met the poets Innokenty Annensky and Anna Akhmatova, the latter of which he was to marry in 1910. The same year he met Akhmatova he published his book of verse, *Put konkvistadorov* (The Path of Conquistadors).

In 1907–1908 Gumilev studied at the Sorbonne in Paris and traveled to Egypt and the Sudan. *Romanticheski tsvety* (Romantic Flowers) appeared the following year. In 1909 he helped to found and edit the literary journal *Apollon*. He also traveled to Abyssinia.

With his marriage to Akhmatova, Gumilev founded the Poets' Guild, which was to last until 1914, expressing the anti-symbolist poetics of his own writing, Akhmatova's and others. The publication of *Chuzhoe nebo* (Foreign Skies) further articulated his Acmeist concerns: balance, precision, craftsmanship, respect for tradition, restraint and clarity.

Throughout this period Gumilev continued to travel, despite the birth of his son Lev, to Italy, Abyssinia again and Somaliland under the auspices of the Russian Academy of Sciences to study East African tribes. He also contined to translate, most notably the poems of Théophile Gautier.

Kolchan (The Quiver) and *Shator* (The Tent) appeared in 1916 and 1921, and reiterated his concerns for the artistic personality and his fascination with African culture.

During World War I Gumilev fought in Prussia and Poland and served on the staff of the Russian Expeditionary Corps in Paris. Returning to Russia in 1918, he divorced Akhmatov, publishing his sixth book of poetry, *Kostyor* (The Pyre) and translating Samuel Coleridge's *Rime of the Ancient Mariner*.

In 1919 he married Anna Engelhardt, who bore him a daughter, Elena, in 1920. The following year Gumilev, active as a poet, translator and editor, was arrested for alleged participation in an anti-Soviet conspiracy, for which he was executed in 1921.

BOOKS OF POETRY:

Put konkvistadorov (Petersburg, 1905); *Romanticheskie tsvety* (Paris, 1908); *Zhemchuga* (Moscow: Skorpion, 1910); *Chuzhoe nebo* (Petersburg: Izdatel'stvo Apollona, 1912); *Kolchan* (Moscow-Petersburg: Giperborei, 1916); *Kostyor* (Petersburg: Giperborei, 1918); *Mik: Afrikanskaya poema* (Petersburg: Giperborei, 1918); *Farforovyi pavil'on* (Petersburg: Giperborei, 1918); *Ognennyi stolp* (Petersburg: Petropolis, 1921); *Shator* (Petersburg: Tsekh poetov, 1921); *K sinyei zvezde* (Ber-

93

lin: Petropolis 1923); *Stikhotvoreniya. Posmertnyi sbornik* (Petersburg: Mysl', 1922); *Stikhotvoreniya i poémy* (Leningrad, 1988).

ENGLISH LANGUAGE TRANSLATIONS:

The Abinger Garland. Nicolai Gumilev. Poems Translated from the Russian, translated by Yakov Hornstein (Dorking, England: Tanner, 1945); *Selected Works of Nikolai S. Gumilev,* translated by Burton Raffel and Alla Burago [Russian Literature in Translation Series, edited by Sidney Monas] (Albany: State University of New York Press, 1972).

Sixth Sense

Fine the wine that loves us,
Good bread baked for our sakes
And the women who torment and tease
Yet please us and in the end let us take them.

But what do we do with the red
Hue of sunset that lets the sky grow cold
With blue in a still, strange serenity?
What to do with a poetry that lives forever.

You can't eat or drink or even kiss
The color of a setting sun or sound
Of poetic line; even as we wring our hands
And try to grab it quick, beauty flies.

As the boy sometimes watching girls bathing
In a lake forgets what he was playing at
And knowing nothing of love sublime
Is tormented by mysterious desires,

As in the primal jungle of the world where
Some mud covered creature, wet and bare
First felt upon his shoulders wings
Unfurled, and in helpless fear howled

Into dense veldt; so through the centuries—
O God, how long?—under nature's knife
art, the soul cries out
of its pale, trembling flesh—from some sixth sense.

—Translated from the Russian by Douglas Messerli

The Streetcar That Lost Its Way

While walking down a strange street
I suddenly heard the cawing of crows,
Distant thunder, and the tones of a lute —
Here came a streetcar flying past.

How I managed to leap to its step
Is beyond me — even in the bright
Daylight it spewed behind itself
In the atmosphere a trail of fire.

It moved forth like a dark, winged storm,
This streetcar losing itself among
The depths of time — "Conductor, stop!
Conductor, stop this car at once!"

Too late. By now we had already
Rounded the wall, crossed through a grove
Of palms, and thundered across three bridges
Over the Neva, the Nile, the Seine.

Then, his face flashing by outside,
An old bum peered in through the window —
He was, of course, the one who died
In Beirut just a year ago.

Where is this? Answering, my heart
Beats listless yet anxiously:
"Is this the station where you buy
Your way to the India of the Soul?"

A billboard: drawn in blood, the letters
"Grocer's"; here, I know, instead
Of cabbages and rutabagas
One may purchase lifeless heads.

And then the executioner,
In red shirt, with face like an udder,
Chopped off my head: it lay with others
In this slimy box, just at the bottom.

Down the alley, a wooden fence,
a house with three windows, and a gray lawn.
"Conductor, stop the car at once!
Conductor, stop the streetcar!"

Mashenka, here you lived and sang,
Wove rugs for me, whom you would wed.
Where is your body, the voice that sang?
Is it possible you are dead?

How you wept inside your room,
While I, with powder in my hair,
Went off the present myself to the Empress,
And never beheld you again.

Now I see it all: Our freedom
Is just a small light breaking through
From another world: people and shadows
Loiter by the gate to the planets' zoo.

A lush, familiar wind begins
To blow, and beyond the bridge, the hand
Of a rider in a glove of iron
And two horses's hooves come flying on.

The great stronghold of Orthodoxy,
St. Isaac's dome, commands the sky.
A prayer of intercession for Mashenka,
Her health; a requiem for me.

But still my heart is always shadowed;
It's hard to breathe; it hurts to live.
Mashenka, I never thought that one could
Have such love, or feel such grief.

—Translated from the Russian by Denis Johnson and Kathy Lewis

Pre-Memory

So this is all of life! Whirling, singing.
Oceans, metropolises, deserts,
A desultory reflection
Of what is lost forever.

A flame rages, trumpets trumpet,
And chestnut-colored horses race,
Then the agitating lips
Of happiness, it seems, repeat.

And sorrow and joy, now again,
Again, as before, as always,
The ocean gestures a gray mane,
Deserts, cities arise.

But when, at last, arising
From sleep, will I again be me—
Just a simple Indian, dozing
On a hallowed evening, by a stream?

—Translated from the Russian by Denis Johnson and Kathy Lewis

A Baby Elephant

Right now my love for you is a baby elephant
Born in Berlin or in Paris,
And treading with its cushioned feet
Around the zoo director's house.

Do not offer it French pastries,
Do not offer it cabbage heads,
It can eat only sections of tangerines,
Or lumps of sugar and pieces of candy.

Don't cry, my sweet, because it will be put
Into a narrow cage, become a joke for mobs,
When salesmen blow cigar smoke into its trunk
To the cackles of their girl friends.

Don't imagine, my dear, that the day will come
When, infuriated, it will snap its chains
And rush along the streets,
Crushing howling people like a bus.

No, may you dream of it at dawn,
Clad in bronze and brocade and ostrich feathers,
Like that magnificent beast which once
Bore Hannibal to trembling Rome.

—Translated from the Russian by Carl R. Proffer

Words

In the old days, when God cast down
His gaze upon the just created earth,
Words stopped the sun,
Words tore down whole towns.

The terror-striken stars
huddled round the moon
When words, like pink flaming tongues
Floated down through air.

The lower levels of beings,
Like domestic cows yoked
Were given numbers, since numbers
Suggest so many things.

The gray old patriach who'd brought
All of good and evil under hand,
Was careful not to make a sound,
So drew a number in the sand.

Thus we forget that only words
Stay brilliant in the light
Of everyday adversity. In Saint John
We find words are God himself.

We have limited what they might have meant
By the shallow shell of our lives,
And like bees in a dried-out hive,
left our rotten smelling words behind.

—Translated from the Russian by Douglas Messerli

Peter Huchel [East Germany (DDR)/now Germany] 1903–1981

Born in Lichterfelde, Berlin, Peter Huchel spent most of his childhood in the German country at the home of his grandfather Mark Brandenburg. And his poetry is infused with his love of the natural world around Brandenburg.

As a young man he attended Humboldt University, the University of Freiburg, and the University of Vienna, studying philosophy and German literature. After school, he survived as a farm worker in France and traveled extensively through the Balkans and Turkey before returning to Berlin.

His first poems, which begin to appear in the 1920s, were associated with the German "Naturlyrik," which presents nature in loving detail and specific description. But gradually, through his social concerns of the poor and lower classes, Huchel's work moved to a more meditative writing on the nature of human existence and survival. This transformation came about, in part, from his serving as a conscript in the German army from 1940 to 1945. Huchel was sent to the Eastern Front, where he was captured by the Russians. At the end of the war, he was taken to the Soviet Zone of Berlin and worked for the radio station there.

His first published volume of poetry, *Gedichte*, appeared in 1948. In 1949, he became the editor of the East German journal *Sinn und Form*, which he helped to transform into one of the most controversial cultural journals in all of Europe. Publishing the likes of Mann, Sartre, Brecht, Brobrowki, and Neruda, the journal withstood the pressures of the Socialist government and represented an exciting interchange of ideological positions.

But Huchel's refusal to remain within the Socialist Party program ultimately gained attention, and in 1962 he was dismissed as the editor; the East German authorities refused to publish his poetry. His second volume of writing, *Chausseen, Chaussen: Gedichte* (Roads, Roads: Poems) was published in the West by S. Fischer Verlag in 1963. Other important volumes, such as *Die nuente Stunde: Gedichte* (The Ninth Hour: Poems), were also published by West German publishers.

In 1977 Huchel suffered a serious illness and was unable to finish his long awaited book of memoirs. He died in 1981.

BOOKS OF POETRY:

Gedichte (Aufbau Verlag, 1948); *Chausseen, Chaussen: Gedichte* (Frankfurt: S. Fischer, 1963); *Die Sternenreuse: Gedichte, 1925-1947* (Munich: Piper, 1967); *Gezaehlte Tage* (Frankfurt: Suhrkamp, 1972); *Ausgewaehlte Gedichte* (Frankfurt: Suhrkamp, 1973); *Unbewohnbar die Trauer* (sound recording) (St.Gallen, 1978); *Die neunte Stunde: Gedichte* (Frankfurt: Suhrkamp, 1979); *Gesammelte Werke in zwei Banden*, edited by Axel Vieregg (Frankfurt: Suhrkamp, 1984).

ENGLISH LANGUAGE TRANSLATIONS:

Selected Poems, translated by Michael Hamburger (Manchester: Carcanet Press, 1974); *The Garden of Theophrastus and Other Poems*, translated by Michael Hamburger (Manchester: Carcanet Press/Dublin: Raven Press, 1983); *A Thistle in His Mouth*, translated by Henry Beissel (Cormorant Books, 1988).

Summer

O nostrils of the dust!
Fiery maw of August
sucking in ponds!

The wind's
nicked scythe
glows in the reeds.

In the crackling shade
of brooding sheaves
Summer crouches,
his bare foot
ripped by stubble.

You I will praise,
Earth,
under the stone slab even,
the silence of a world
without sleep or permanence.

—*Translated from the German by Michael Hamburger*

(from *Gedichte,* 1948)

The Sign

Hill bare of trees,
once again at evening
the flight of wild ducks passed
through watery autumn air.

Was it the sign?
With pale yellow lances
the lake pierced
unquiet mist.

I walked through the village
and saw what I expected.
The shepherd held a ram
wedged between his knees.

He pared the hoof,
he tarred the stubble lameness.
And women counted the pails,
the day's milking.
There was nothing to interpret.
The accounts had been kept.

Only the dead,
removed from the hourly stroke
of the bell, the ivy's growth,
they see
the icy shadow of earth
slide over the moon.
They know that this will remain.
After all that breathes
in air and water.

Who wrote
the warning words,
hardly to be deciphered?
I found them on the post,
near the lake's far shore.
Was it the sign?

Frozen
in the silence of snow
the viper thicket
blindly slept.

—Translated from the German by Michael Hamburger

(from *Chausseen, Chausseen*, 1963)

San Michele

At the corner of the wall
a black fire
that warms the way home of the dead.
While the shadow of their prayers
wafts over sleeping waters
a bell
you cannot hear swings.

Every hour moves through your heart
and the last kills.

Yesterday,
under the almond trees
they set fire
to the dry grass.
Ransom yourself
in view of the pit.

Night, that dark blood-letting,
seeps into the lead of roofs.
Distant Venice
is not worth a catch of fish.

—Translated from the German by Michael Hamburger

(from *Chausseen, Chausseen*, 1963)

Roads

Choked sunset glow
of crashing time.
Roads. Roads.
Intersections of flight.
Cart tracks across the ploughed field
that with the eyes
of killed horses
saw the sky in flames.

Nights with lungs full of smoke,
with the hard breath of the fleeing
when shots
struck the dusk.
Out of a broken gate
ash and wind came without a sound,
a fire
that sullenly chewed the darkness.

Corpses,
flung over the rail tracks,
their stifled cry
like a stone on the palate.

A black
humming cloth of flies
closed over wounds.

—Translated from the German by Michael Hamburger

(from *Chausseen, Chausseen,* 1963)

Dream in the Steel Trap

You are caught, dream.
Your ankle sears,
smashed in the steel trap.

Wind turns the page
of a piece of bark.
Opened up
is the testament of fallen spruces,
written
in rain-grey patience
ineffaceable
its last will—
silence.

Hail chisels
the inscription on to the black smoothness
of a puddle.

—Translated from the German by Michael Hamburger

(from *Chausseen, Chausseen,* 1963)

On the Death of V. W.

She forgot about the ash
on the warped piano keys,
the flickering light in the windows.

It began with a pond,
then came the pebbly path,
the railed well, with mugwort around it,
the leaky drinking-trough under the elm tree
where the horses used to stand.

Then came night
that was like falling water.
At times, for hours,
a bird spirit,
half buzzard, half swan,
just above the rushes
from which a snow-storm howls.

—Translated from the German by Michael Hamburger

(from *Chausseen, Chausseen*, 1963)

Macbeth

I talked with witches,
in what language,
I don't remember.

Blasted open
the gates of Heaven,
the spirit unleashed,
in whirlwinds
the heath folk.

By the sea
the dirty toes of the snow,
here waits a man
with skinless hands.
I wish my mother
had suffocated me.

From the stables of the wind
he will come
where the old women
chop up chaff for fodder.

Suspicion, my helmet,
I'll hang it up
on the rafters of night.

—Translated from the German by Michael Hamburger

(from *Chausseen, Chausseen*, 1963)

The Street

March midnight, the gardener said,
on our way from the station,
as we saw the rear light of a late train
fade out in the fog. Somebody walked behind us,
we talked of the weather.
The wind hurls rain
on to the ice of the ponds,
slowly the year is turning into the light.

And all that night
a roar in the keyholes.
The grassblade's fury
lashes the earth.
And around daybreak light
churns up the dark.
The pines rake fog from the window-panes.

Down there, wretched
as tobacco smoke left behind,
stands my neighbor, the shadow
that trails my feet, if I leave the house.
Glumly yawning
in the bare trees' drizzle
today he's tinkering with rusty wire on the fence.
What's it worth to him, if he notes the accusing facts
in his blue exercise book, the car numbers of my friends,
keeps an eye on a street so vulnerable,
on the contraband,
forbidden books,
crumbs for our stomachs,
concealed in coat linings.
A single twig thrown on a feeble fire.

I have not come
to churn up the dark.
Nor will I scatter in front of my threshold
the ash of my verses
to keep evil spirits out.

This morning
with damp fog
on its Prussian-Saxon uniform,
with fading lights on the frontier,

the State a mattock,
the people a thistle,
I descend as usual
the decrepit stairs.

In the room I see my son
decipher the Ugaritic text
of Ras Shamra's cuneiform,
the bracketing
of dream and life,
the peaceable campaign of King Keret.
On the seventh day
as IL the god proclaims,
came hot air to drink dry the wells,
the dogs howled,
the donkeys cried out with thirst.
And no battering ram was needed to make a city surrender.

—Translated from the German by Michael Hamburger

(from *Chausseen, Chausseen*, 1963)

Meeting

Barn owl,
daughter of snow,
subject to the night wind,

yet taking root
with her talons
in the rotten scab of walls,

beak face
with round eyes,
heart-rigid mask
of feathers that are a white fire
touching neither time nor space,

coldly the night blows
at the old homestead,
in its yard pale folk,
sledges, baggage, lamps covered with snow,

in the pots death,
in the pitchers poison,
the last will nailed to a post.

The hidden thing
under the rocks' claws,
the opening into night,
terror of death
thrust into flesh like stinging salt.

Let us go down
in the language of angels
to the broken bricks of Babel.

—Translated from the German by Michael Hamburger

(from *Die neunte Stunde*, 1979)

At Bud

By night
the dry coughing along the corridor.
I open the door
and inhale the net smell of the old man
who was left under the cliffs.

The sea writes
in seaweed script
the last page of the logbook
on to salty rocks—
renounce your homecoming,
be on your way
on oceans with a falling skyline
where every name is lost.

—Translated from the German by Michael Hamburger

(from *Die neunte Stunde*, 1979)

By Night

Above the clouds
the creaking of cartwheels,
fugitives
on their way.

Sturdy fellows
clear away the fog,
carry sleeping women
across the ford.

Rushes,
hardly discernible.
A man,
with a dragnet flung over his shoulders,
stands by the water
and guts the fishes.

Scars
the fishes' gills,
they gleam in moonlight.

The word, sown for the night,
germinates, roots in the wind.
Unending
the litany of the rain.

—Translated from the German by Michael Hamburger

(from *Die neunte Stunde*, 1979)

PERMISSIONS

"Summer," "The Sign," "San Michele," "Roads," "Dream of the Steel Trap," "On the Death of V. W.,"
"Macbeth," "The Street," "Meeting," "At Bud," and "Night"
Reprinted from *The Garden of Theophrastus and Other Poems*, Peter Huchel, trans. by Michael Hamburger
(Manchester, England: Carcanet Press/Dublin: Raven Press, 1983). Translation copyright ©1983 by Michael
Hamburger. Reprinted by permission of Michael Hamburger.

Vicente Huidobro [Vicente García Fernández] [Chile] 1893–1948

Vicente Huidobro

Hans Arp

Born in Santiago, Chile in 1893, Huidobro was educated at a Jesuit school, which later led to a profound spiritual crisis in the young man, as he revolted against his aristocratic Roman Catholic upbringing. He left for Paris in 1916, having published six books of poetry. Although the first four books had little new to offer, he had moved in the last years of his youth to develop the ideas, most clearly in *Adán*, which Pierre Reverdy, Huidobro and others in Paris would describe as "creationism."

Once in Paris, Huidobro (the pseudonym he had created for himself) began to contribute to the avant-garde literary magazines, particulary *Sic* and *Nord-Sud*, which he co-edited with Reverdy and Guillaume Apollinaire. During these early years he published six further books of poetry, including *Horizon Carré, Tour Eiffel,* and *Hallali*. Travel to Madrid in 1918 brought the attention of the Spanish avant-gardists such as Gerardo Diego, Juan Larrea, and Jorge Luis Borges, who encouraged him. The result of this interchange was Ultraism, which would, in turn, influence the young Argentine poet, Oliverio Girondo.

Huidobro returned to Chile for one year in 1925, and became the editor of a newspaper and ran as candidate for the Chilean Federation of Students in the national elections. Upon his defeat, Huidobro returned to France, where he continued his writing, including several novels and other works in other genres.

In 1936 he participated in the Spanish Civil War on the side of the Republic. As the fall of the Republic became imminent, he returned to Chile, where he wrote his important satrical novel, *Sátiro; o, El poder de las palabras* (1939).

Huidobro's major poetic work was his long poem, *Altazor*, subtitled "Journey in a Parachute," published in Madrid in 1931. Like Joyce and other major avant-gardists, Huidobro's work is made up of a complex layering of word-play and puns. Even the title relates to the root words: *alto* (high), *Azor* (goshawk), while at the same, through its subtitle, suggesting the Icarus-like possibilities of the fall.

The poet's last two works, *Ver y palpar* (1941) and *El ciudadano del olvido* (1941) contain autobiographal and personal elements. He died in Cartagena in 1948.

BOOKS OF POETRY:

Ecos del alma (Santiago: Imprenta Chile, 1911); *Canciones en la noche* (Santiago: Imprenta Chile, 1913); *La gruta de silencio* (Santiago: Imprenta Chile, 1913); *Las pagodas ocultas* (Santiago: Imprenta Universitaría, 1914); *Adán* (Santiago: Imprenta Universitaría, 1916); *El espejo de agua* (Buenos Aires: Editorial Orión, 1916); *Horizon Carré* (Paris: Editions Paul Birault, 1917); *Tour Eiffel* (Madrid: Imprenta Pueyo, 1918); *Hallali* (Madrid: Ediciones Jesús López, 1918); *Ecuatorial* (Madrid: Imprenta Pueyo, 1918); *Poemas articos* (Madrid: Imprenta Pueyo, 1918); *Saisons choisies* (Paris:

Editions Le Cible, 1921); *Automne régulier* (Paris: Editions Librairie de France, 1925); *Tout à Coup* (Paris: Editions Au Sans Pareil, 1925); *Altazor: el viaje en paracaídas* (Madrid: Campañía Iberoamericana de Publications, 1931); *Temblor de cielo* (Madrid: Editorial Plutarco, 1931); *Ver y palpar* (Santiago: Ediciones Ercilla, 1941); *El ciudadano del olvido* (Santiago: Ediciones Ercilla, 1941); *Antología de Vicente Huidobro* (Santiago: Editorial Zig-Zag, 1945); *Ultimos poemas* (Santiago: Talleres Gráficos Ahués, 1948); *Poesías*, edited with a prologue by Enrique Lihn (Havana: Casa de las Américas, 1968); *Obras Completas de Vicente Huidobro* (Santiago: Editorial Zig-Zag, 1964); *Obras Completas de Vicente Huidobro* (Santiago: Editorial Andres Bello, 1976)

ENGLISH LANGUAGE TRANSLATIONS:

The Relativity of Spring: 13 poems translated from the French, translated by Michael Palmer and Geoffrey Young (Berkeley, California: Sand Dollar, 1976); *The Selected Poetry of Vicente Huidobro*, edited by David Guss (New York: New Directions, 1981); *Altazor*, translated by Eliot Weinberger (Saint Paul, Minnesota: Graywolf Press, 1988); *The Poet Is a Little God: Creationist Verse*, translated by Jorge García-Gómez (Riverside, California: Xenos Books, 1990).

Ars Poetica

Let the verse be as a key
Opening a thousand doors.
A leaf falls; something is flying by;
Let whatever your eyes gaze upon be created,
And the soul of the hearer remain shivering.

Invent new worlds and watch over your word;
The adjective, when not a life-giver, kills.

We are in the cycle of nerves.
Like a memory
The muscle hangs in the museums;
Nevertheless, we have no less strength:
True vigor
Dwells in the head.

Why do you sing the rose, oh Poets!
Make it blossom in the poem;

Only for us
Live all things under the Sun.

The Poet is a little God.

—*Translated from the Spanish by Jorge García-Gómez*

(from *Espejo de Agua*, 1916)

Cow Boy
for Jacques Lipchitz

In the Far West
       where there is only one moon
The Cok Boy sings
       until it breaks the night
And his cigar is a wandering star
      HIS PONY SHOED WITH WINGS
      HAS NEVER HAD A FLAW
And him
     his head against his knees

Woodcut by Hans Arp

                    he dances a Cake Walk
New York
        a few kilometers

In the skyscrapers
The elevators rise like thermometers

And near Niagara
                which has put out my pipe
I watch the spattered stars

The Cow Boy
            on a violin string
Crosses the Ohio

> —*Translated from the French by David M. Guss*

(from *Horizon Carré*, 1917)

Child

That house
            Sitting on Time
Over the clouds
                carried away by the wind
Went a dead bird

Its feathers fall on autumn

A wingless child   The sloop is sliding

Looks out the window   And beneath the shadow of its masts

                            The fish are afraid of shredding the water

The mother's name is forgotten

Behind the door
            which is clapping like a flag

The roof is drilled by stars

                    The grandfather is asleep

Some snow
        Falls from his beard

—Translated from the Spanish by Jorge García-Gómez

(from *Poemas articos*, 1918)

Sailor

That bird flying for the first time
Goes away from the nest looking backward

With my finger on my lips
                I have summoned you

I invented water games
For tree tops

I made you the most beautiful of women
So beautiful you would blush in the afternoons

                The moon leaves us
                And throws a crown over the pole

I made rivers flow
                that never had existed

With a shout I raised a mountain
And around it we danced a new dance

                I cut all the roses
                From the clouds of the east

I taught a snow bird to sing

Let's walk over the unraveled months

I am the old sailor
                Who stitches together severed horizons

—Translated from the Spanish by Cola Franzen

(from *Poemas articos*, 1918)

from *Altazor*

CANTO III

Break the loops of veins
The links of breath and the chains

Of eyes paths of horizons
Flower screened on uniform skies

Soul paved with recollections
Like stars carved by the wind

The sea is a roof of bottles
That dreams in the sailor's memory

The sky is that pure flowing hair
Braided by the hands of the aeronaut

And the airplane carries a new language
To the mouth of the eternal skies

Chains of glances tie us to the earth
Break them break so many chains

The first man flies to light the sky
Space bursts open in a wound

And the bullet returns to the assassin
Forever tied to the infinite

Cut all the links
Of river sea and mountain

Of spirit and memory
Of dying law and fever dreams

It is the world that turns and goes on and whirls
In the last eyeball

Tomorrow the countryside
Will follow the galloping horses

The flower will suck the bee
For the hangar will be a hive

The rainbow will become a bird
And fly singing to its nest

Crows will become planets
And sprout feathers of grass

Leaves will be loose feathers
Falling from their throats

Glances will be rivers
And the rivers wounds in the legs of space

The flock will guide its shepherd
So the day can doze drowsy as an airplane

And the tree will perch on the turtledove
While the clouds turn to stone

For everything is as it is in every eye
An ephemeral astrological dynasty

Falling from universe to universe

The poet is a manicurist of language
Not the magician who lights and douses
Stellar words and the cherries of vagabond good-byes
Far from the hands of the earth
And everything he says is his invention
Things that move outside the ordinary world
Let us kill the poet who gluts us

Poetry still and poetry poetry
Poetical poetry poetry
Poetical poetry by poetical poets
Poetry
Too much poetry
From the rainbow to the piano-bench ass of the lady next door
Enough poetry bambina enough lady
It still has bars across its eyes
The game is a game and not an endless prayer

Smiles or laughter not the eyeball's little lamps
That wheel from affliction toward the sea
Smiles and gossip of the weaver star
Smiles of a brain evoking dead stars
On the seance table of its radiance

Enough lady harp of the beautiful images
Of furtive illuminated "likes"
It's something else we're looking for something else
We already know how to dart a kiss like a glance
Plant glances like trees
Cage trees like birds
Water birds like heliotropes
Play a heliotrope like music
Empty music like a sack
Decapitate a sack like a penguin
Cultivate penguins like vineyards
Milk a vineyard like a cow
Unmast cows like schooners
Comb a schooner like a comet
Disembark comets like tourists
Charm tourists like snakes
Harvest snakes like almonds
Undress an almond like an athlete
Fell athletes like cypresses
Light cypresses like lanterns
Nestle lanterns like skylarks
Heave skylarks like sighs
Embroider sighs like silks
Drain silks like rivers
Raise a river like a flag
Pluck a flag like a rooster
Douse a rooster like a fire
Row through fires like seas
Reap seas like wheat
Ring wheat like bells
Bleed bells like lambs
Draw lambs like smiles
Bottle smiles like wine
Set wine like jewels
Electrify jewels like sunsets
Man sunsets like battleships
Uncrown a battleship like a king

Hoist kings like dawns
Crucify dawns like prophets
Etc. etc. etc.
Enough sir violin sunk in a wave wave
Everyday wave of misery religion
Of dream after dream possession of jewels
After the heart-eating roses
And the nights of the perfect ruby
The new athlete leaps on the magic track
Frolicking with magnetic words
Hot as the earth when a volcano rises
Hurling the sorceries of his bird phrases

The last poet withers away
The bells of the continents chime
The moon dies with the night on its back
The sun pulls the day out of its pocket
The solemn new land opens its eyes
And moves from earth to the stars
The burial of poetry

All the languages are dead
Dead in the hands of the tragic neighbor
We must revive the languages
With raucous laughter
With wagonloads of giggles
With circuit breakers in the sentences
And cataclysm in the grammar
Get up and walk
Stretch your legs limber the stiff joints
Fires of laughter for the shivering language
Astral gymnastics for the numb tongues
Get up and walk
Live live like a football
Burst in the mouth of motorcycle diamonds
In the drunkenness of its fireflies
The very vertigo of its liberation
A beautiful madness in the life of the word
A beautiful madness in the zone of language
Adventure lined with tangible disdain
The adventure of language between two wrecked ships
A delightful catastrophe on the rails of verse

And since we must live and not kill ourselves
As long as we live let us play
The simple sport of words
Of the pure word and nothing more
Without images awash with jewels
(Words carry too much weight)
A ritual of shadowless words
An angel game there in the infinite
Word by word
By the light of a star that a crash brings to life
Sparks leap from the crash and then more violent
More enormous is the explosion
Passion of the game in space
With no moon-wings no pretense
Single combat between chest and sky
Total severance at last of voice and flesh
Echo of light bleeding air into the air

Then nothing nothing
Spirit whisper of the wordless phrase

—Translated from the Spanish by Eliot Weinberger

(from *Altazor*, 1931)

Maruyama Kaoru [Japan]
1899–1974

Maruyama Kaoru

Maruyama Kaoru is read little today in Japan or abroad, in part because of Japanese readers' dismissal of him as an "intellectual" poet and because much of his work has been unfairly labeled as "sea-poetry." Maruyama did attempt to check lyricism and sentimentality in his work, and due to his life-long fascination with the sea, he wrote a great many poems about the ocean and voyages; but his work overall is quite varied and the controlled surface of his works often is belied by highly emotional content.

Born into the family of a high ranking bureaucrat, Maruyama spent much of his early years adapting to new surroundings, as his father was transferred numerous times to different locations. In the tightly-knit social structures of Japan, such displacement obviously had its effects; throughout his life Maruyama felt separated and apart from the Tokyo-centered poetry circles.

Living in the port of Yokohama in 1911, he was taken on class trip to see the ships in the harbor. The blue eyes of the Scandinavian sailors amazed the young boy, and from that incident, Maruyama dates his fascination with the sea. Despite strong opposition from his family, he sat for the entrance examination to the Merchant Marine Academy. Failing the examination, he enrolled in Tokyo preparatory school in order to retake the tests the following year. In 1918 he passed the exam and entered the academy.

However, at the academy his dreams of becoming a ship captain were dashed as he discovered his fear of heights; the intense physical activity of the Academy, moreover, caused his legs to swell, and he received a medical release. Under his mother's guidance, he took the examination of the Third Higher School in Kyoto, where he entered in 1921 in French literature. By the time he entered Tokyo University in 1926, he had already determined to become a poet. Influenced by the works of Edgar Allan Poe, Oscar Wilde and others, including the Japanese master Hagiwara Sakutarō, Maruyama determined to use his education as literary stimulus rather than as a goal towards a bachelor's degree.

During this period he met Takai Miyoko, with whom he fell in love and married in 1928. Upon their marriage he rented a luxurious residence in Tokyo and later invited his mother to move in with them. He also dropped out of the university to concentrate on writing.

The collapse of the Japanese economy in 1930 meant difficult times for the family. Forced to move again and again, Maruyama found it difficult to concentrate on writing. But in 1931, his wife found a job in downtown Tokyo with sufficient pay to support his concentration on his art. His first collection, *Ho—Ranpu—Kamome* (Sail—Lamp—Gull) appeared in 1932. Soon after, he joined with other poets in publishing *Shiki* (Four Seasons), which involved him, for the first time, in the Tokyo poetry circles, and helped in the development of his poetic aesthetic. In particular, the theory of his fellow university student and poet Hori Tatsuo (1904-1953) and the writings of Rainier Maria Rilke highly influenced him in his attempt to balance objective observation and intellectual truths of the mind.

In 1935 he published two books, *Tsuru no Sôshiki* (Funeral of the Crane) and *Yônen* (Infancy). The second book won the *Bungei Hanron* poetry prize, which brought much needed money and request for new manuscripts.

The following year, however, tragedy struck as his sister-in-law, with whom had developed a close friendship, died of consumption. His fourth collection of poetry, *Ichinichishû* (A Single Day) contains a section devoted to her memory.

An invitation to write on midshipmen's experiences at sea finally realized Maruyama's boyhood dream in 1941. Those experiences were collected in poetry in 1943 in *Tenshô naru Tokoro* (Hear the Ship's Bell).

The Japanese war effort disrupted Maruyama's activities in the years following, and in 1945 he and his family escaped into the "snow country" of the north, where he remained until 1948, when he moved to his wife's home city of Toyohashi at the age of fifty. There he settled into a lectureship on modern Japanese poetry and began to write the books of his last years: *Seishun Fuzai* (1952, Lost Youth), *Tsuresarareta Umi* (1962, The Hostage Sea), *Tsuki Wataru* (1972, Moon Passage), and *Ari no iru Kao* (1973, Face with Ants). He died of cerebral thrombosis at the age of 75 in October 1974.

BOOKS OF POETRY:

Ho—Ranpu—Kamome (Daiichi Shobô, 1932); *Tsuru no Sôshiki* (Daiichi Shobô, 1935); *Yônen* (Shiki Sha, 1935); *Ichinichishû* (Hangasô, 1936); *Busshô Shishû* (Kawade Shobô, 1941); *Namida shita Kami* (Usui Shobô, 1942); *Tenshô naru Tokoro* (Ooka Sha, 1943); *Tsuyoi Nippon* (Kokumin Tosho Kankôkai, 1944) [author refused to acknowlege this work]; *Kitaguni* (Usui Shobô, 1946); *Senkyô* (Sapporo Seiji Sha, 1948); *Aoi Kokuban* (Nyûfurendo Sha, 1948); *Hana no Shin* (Sôgen Sha, 1948); *Seishun Fuzai* (Sôgen Sha, 1952); *Tsuresarareta Umi* (Chôryû Sha, 1962); *Tsuki Wataru* (Chôryû Sha, 1972); *Ari no iru Kao* (Chûô Kôron Sha, 1973); *Maruyama Kaoru Zenshû* (Kadokawa Shoten, 1976-77).

ENGLISH LANGUAGE TRANSLATIONS:

Self-Righting Lamp: Selected Poems, translated by Robert Epp (Rochester, Michigan: Katydid Books, 1990).

Into Clouds on the Hill

I pet my dog
neck to back
back to tail

Ears lie flat
Coat glistening
belly bent in a bow

Ah my petting hand   wind in motion
the dog's stance bending into my strokes
the dog's dashing through its stance

I unleash him into clouds on the hill
The dog bounds off full speed
like a flung stone you can't call back

—*Translated from the Japanese by Robert Epp*

(from *Busshô Shishû*, 1941)

Into the Future

The father said:
Look! at this picture
at the sleigh dashing swiftly on
at the wolf pack in pursuit
see the reinsman frantically whipping the reindeer
see the traveler taking steady aim with a rifle
from behind the luggage
now a scarlet flash from the muzzle

The son said:
One wolf's downed   right?
Oh another sprang at the sleigh
but tumbled over backward covered with blood
It's night the endless steppes buried in snow
Can the traveler hold out?
How far has the sleigh to go?

The father said:

The sleigh flies like this till dawn
slaying yesterday's regrets one by one
dashing like Time into tomorrow
Soon beyond the path that sun will climb
streets of the future will glimmer into view
Look!
Sky on the hill already turning white

—*Translated from the Japanese by Robert Epp*

(from *Namida shita Kami,* 1942)

A Poet's Words

The late Nakahara Chûya said
"You find no mermaids in the sea
In the sea
are only waves"

These words from some strange reason
remain vivid in my mind
If I chant them three times
mermaid faces peer out from between the sounds
If I mutter these words to myself
as I think back on a past cruise through southern seas
countless mermaid arms and tails appear and disappear
into sea's high blue swells

Or if I think dreamily of these words
when standing on a rock shore under overcast skies
splashes of foam that dash against crags
sound like mermaid's sighing

The late Nakahura Chûya's legacy to me:
The word *wave* has become mermaid
The word *mermaid*
has become wave

—*Translated from the Japanese by Robert Epp*

(from *Tenshô naru Tokoro,* 1943)

Carossa and Rilke

In his *Romanian Diary*
Carossa wrote as follows
about a young girl suffering from consumption
in the aftermath of war's destruction
  "The scant oxygen in her entire body seemed
    concentrated in those hugely opened eyes"
If at that moment
he had inadvertanly approached her with the flame of love
her eyes would have burnt away in an instant
and she would have gone to heaven

They say Rilke's eyes were always limpidly blue
profoundly absorbing imagery
without harboring even a hint of a shadow
What if we had sailed a boat on a lake of that hue?
Dread would quickly have driven us insane

—*Translated from the Japanese by Robert Epp*

(from *Hana no Shin*, 1948)

News from the Cape

Over the last two or three days here
the sea has been intensely transparent
the sky pure blue

Turning up my heels
each day I dive
deep into the sea and
marvelous! marvelous!
before I know it I'm in the sky
Through my diving goggles
I can see the sun between a cleft in the rocks

Holding my spear high
I rush toward the light
Then somewhere
a harp starts singing serenely
and a file of fish circles the sky
as in an ancient Egyptian mural

Reaching out gingerly
I pry off sea mussels and abalone
from behind the sun

—*Translated from the Japanese by Robert Epp*

(from *Seishun Fuzai*, 1952)

A Crane

A crane soars
over the blue sea

like a sooted and shabby umbrella
singing sadly

That bubble reputation
so long enjoyed
turns to shadow   slips away
mirrored black
on creases in the brine.

—*Translated from the Japanese by Robert Epp*

(from *Maruyama Kaoru Zenshû*, written 1955)

The Tree in Me

I don't know when it began but a tree has taken root in me
It grows through my growth
Spreading branches from my growing limbs
its leaves thicken into shapes of grief

I no longer go out
I no longer speak to anyone
not to Mother not even to firends...
I'm becoming the tree in me
No no I've already become that tree

I stand quietly far beyond the fields

Whenever I greet morning sun
whenever I look off after clouds fired by sunset
my silence glitters
my solarity self sings

—Translated from the Japanese by Robert Epp

(from *Maruyama Kaoru Zenshû*, written 1956)

Illusion in the Reef

The chalk coral grove
comes floating transparently to the surface
like a sunken image
deep within a poem
A single baby shark undulates
through coral tips sunlight streaming everywhere
No that's a boot
an airman's book already beginning to dissolve
like a shadow like kelp

—Translated from the Japanese by Robert Epp

(from *Tsuresarareta Umi*, 1962)

Minato Ward, Nagoya (Memo on the Isé Bay Typhoon)

Mackerel bob up from the kitchen
enter the alleyway through a window and   revived
swim down the street between slanting utility poles
heading vigorously for the estuary for the sea
Deep under riled-up eddying waters
    women
    children
    old people
who had instantly exchanged their souls with the fish
surface here and there and   towed off on rafts
pass again today
under twilight eaves holding their breath
Tomorrow cremation under sunny skies

—Translated from the Japanese by Robert Epp

(from *Ari no iru Kao*, 1973)

Face with Ants

Ants crawl over eyelids
Then that nearby hollow suddenly gathers shadows
as though engraved

Ants lick the inner corners of the eyes
From there they go straight down the cheek
—and as I watch   that nearby hollow
deepens as though scooped out

Ants circle that mole by the mouth
Then they scurry into breathless nostrils
They won't show themselves again
They may never reappear

Oh the shame of staring so
Oh the shame of being so stared at

—Translated from the Japanese by Robert Epp

(from *Ari no iru Kao*, 1973)

Pablo Neruda [Chile]
1904–1973

Pablo Neruda

Born in Parral, Chile, Pablo Neruda has long been considered one of the most important Spanish American poets of the 20th century. He won the Nobel Prize for literature in 1971.

His early youth was spent in the small town of Temuco, and later he attended schools in the capital city of Santiago. He studied French at the University of Santiago.

He began writing poetry early, including the highly-praised *Viente poems de amor y una canción desesperada* (1924, *Twenty Love Poems and a Song of Despair*), *La canción de la fiesta* (1921), and *Crepusculario* (1923).

Soon after graduating, Neruda obtained an appointment in the Chilean diplomatic service, and was sent to Rangoon, Burma. It was there and elsewhere in the Far East that he completed the first volume of his great collection *Residencia en la tierra* (1933, *Residence on Earth*). During this period, he became friends with the Spanish poet Federico García Lorca. In 1934 Neruda was assigned as Chilean consul in Barcelona, which brought him closer to García Lorca and other poets of the Generation of 1927, who hailed him a major figure of Hispanic literature. He completed the second volume of *Residencia en la tierra* while in Spain.

The Spanish Civil War changed his life and poetry, as he moved from a personal voice to more politically involved and ideological positions. He participated in leftist politics and became a member of the Chilean Communist Party in 1945. Because of his support of the Soviet Union, particularly while he was consul in Mexico City, he was attacked by pro-Nazi sympathizers, and was stripped of his diplomatic position.

A visit to the Incan ruins of Macchu Picchu in 1943 inspired him to write *Alturas de Macchu Picchu* (1943, *The Heights of Macchu Picchu*), which he later incorporated into his book *Canto general* (1950, general song). The final volume of *Residencia en la tierra* was completed in 1947, containing poems written between 1935 and 1945.

Neruda was elected to the Chilean senate in 1946, but when he denounced the goverment's anticommunist purge, he was indicted and was forced to flee Chile. He traveled extensively until 1952, a time during which he was awarded the Stalin Prize for literature and the Lenin Peace Prize.

He died in Santiago in 1973.

BOOKS OF POETRY:

La canción de la fiesta (Santiago: Federación de Estudiantes de Chile, 1921); *Crepusculario* (Santiago: Nascimento, 1923); *Viente poemas de amor y una canción desesperada* (Santiago: Nascimento); *Anillos* (Santiago: Nascimento, 1926); *Tentativa del hombre infinto* (Santiago: Nascimento, 1926); *El hondero entusiasta, 1923-1924* (Santiago: Ediciones Ercilla, 1933); *Residencia en la tierra* (Madrid: Ediciones del Arbol) [Vol I: 1933; Vol II: 1935]; *Poesías de Yillamediana presentadas por Pablo Naruda* (Madrid: Cruz y Raya, 1935); *Homenaje a Pablo Neruda de los poetas españoles: Tres cantos materiales* (Madrid: Plutarco, 1935); *España en el corazón: himno a las glorias del pueblo en la guerra* (Santiago: Ediciones Ecrilla, 1937); *Las furias y las penas* (Santiago: Nascimento, 1939); *Un canto para Bolívar* (Mexico City: Universidad Nacional Autónoma de México, 1941); *Nuevo canto de amor a Staingrado* (Mexico City: comité de ayuda a Rusia en guerra, 1943); *Canto general de Chile* (privately printed, 1943); *Cantos de Pablo Neruda* (Lima: Hora del Hombre, 1943); *Cántico* (Bogota: La Gran Colombia, 1943); *Pablo Neruda: Sus mejores versos* (Bogota: La Gran Colombia, 1943); *Selección*, edited by Arturo Aldunate (Santiago: Nascimento, 1943); *Saludo al norte de Stalingrado* (privately printed, 1945); *tercera residencia, 1935-1945)* (Buenos Aires, Losada, 1947); *Himno y regreso* (Santiago: Cruz del Sur, 1948); *¡Qué despierte el leñador!* (Havana: Colección Yagruma, 1948); *Colección residencia en la tierra: Obra poética* [10 volumes] (Santiago: Cruz del Sur, 1947-1948); *Alturas de Macchu-Picchu* (Santiago: Librería Neira, 1948) *Canto general* (Mexico City: Cimité Auspiciador, 1950); *Poesías completas* (Buenos Aires: Losada, 1951); *Poemas* (Buenos Aires: Fundamentos, 1952); *Los versos del capitán: Poemas de amor* (Naples: privately printed, 1952); *Todo el amor* (Santiago: Nascimento, 1953); *Las uvas y el viento* (Santiago: Nascimento, 1954); *Odas elementales* (Buenos Aires: Losada, 1954); *Regreso la sirena* (Santiago: Ediciones del Centro de Amigos de Polonia, 1954); *Los versos más populares* (Santiago: Austral, 1954); *Nuevas odas elementales* (Buenos Aires: Losada, 1956); *Oda a la tipografía* (Santiago: Nascimento, 1956); *Los mejores versos de Pablo Neruda* (Buenos Aires: Losada, 1956); *Dos odas elementales* (Buenos Aires: Losada, 1957); *Obras completas* (Buenos Aires: Losada, 1957); *Antología* (Santiago: Nascimento, 1957); *Estravagario* (Buenos Aires: Losada, 1958); *Tercer libro de las odas* (Buenos Aires: Losada, 1959); *Algunas odas* (Santiago: Edición del 55, 1959); *Cien sonetos de amor* (Buenos Aires: 1959); *Odas: Al libro, a las Américas, a la luz* (Caracas: Homenaje de la Asociación de Escritores Venezolanos, 1959); *Todo lleva tu nombre* (Caracas: Ministerio de Educación, 1959); *Navegaciones y regresos* (Buenos Aires: Losada, 1959); *Canción de gesta* (Havana: Imprenta Nacional de Cuba, 1960); *Oceana* (Havana: La Tertulia, 1960); *Los primeros versos de amor* (Santiago: Austral, 1961); *Las piedras de Chile* (Buenos Aires: Losada, 1961); *Cantos ceremoniales* (Buenos Aires: Losada, 1962); *Poema con grabado* [with Mario Toral] (Santiago: Ediciones Isla Negra, 1962); *Memorial de Isla Negra* [5 volumes] (Buenos Aires: Losada, 1964); *Poesías*, selected by Roberto Retamar (Havana: Casa de las Américas, 1965); *Arte de pájaros* (Santiago: Sociedad de Amigos del Arte Contemporáneo, 1966); *Una casa en la arena* (poetry and prose) (Barcelona: Lumen, 1966); *La barcarola* (Buenos Aires, Losada, 1967); *Comiendo en Hungría* [with Miguel Angel Asturias]; *Las manos del día* (Buenos Aires: Losada, 1968); *Aun: Poema* (Santiago: Nascimento, 1969); *Fin de mundo* (Buenos Aires: Losada, 1969); *La copa de sangre* (poetry and prose) (privately printed, 1969); *Las piedras del cielo* (Buenos Aires: Losada, 1970); *Cantos de amor y de combate* (Santiago: Austral, 1971); *Antología esencial*, selected by Hernán Loyola (Buenos Aires: Losada, 1971); *Poemas imortales*, selected by Jaime Concha (Santiago: Quimantu, 1971); *Geografía infructuosa* (Buenos Aires: Losada, 1972); *Cuartros poemas escritos in Francia* (Santiago: Nascimento, 1972); *Libro de las odas* (Buenos Aires: Losada, 1972); *Obras escogidas*, selected by Francisco Coloane (Santiago: A Bello, 1972); *Antología popular 1972* (Santiago, 1972); *El mar y las campanas: Poemas* (Buenos Aires: Losada, 1973); *La rosa separada* (Buenos Aires: Losada, 1973); *El corazón amarillo* (Buenos Aires: Losada, 1974); *Elegía* (Buenos Aires: Losada, 1974); *Defectos escogidos* (Buenos Aires: Losada, 1974); *Oda a la lagartija* (Camp Rico de Canovanas: P. R. Martorell, 1974); *Poesía* [2 volumes] (Barcelona: Noguer, 1974); *Jardín de invierno* (Buenos Aires: Losada, 1974); *Libro de las preguntas* (Buenos Aires: Losada, 1977).

ENGLISH LANGUAGE TRANSLATIONS:

Selected Poems (from *Residencia en la tierra*), translated by Angel Flores (privately printed, 1944); *Residence on Earth and Other Poems*, translated by Angel Flores (New York: New Directions, 1946); *The Selected Poems of Pablo Neruda*, edited and translated by Ben Belitt (New York: Grove Press, 1961); *Twenty Love Poems; A Distaining Song*, translated by W. S. Merwin (New York: Grossman, 1961); *Bestiary/Bestiario: A Poem*, translated by Elsa Neuberger (New York: Harcourt, Brace, 1965); *The Heights of Macchu Picchu*, translated by Nathaniel Tarn (London: Jonathan Cape, 1966; republished by New York: Farrar, Straus, & Giroux, 1967); *We are Many*, translated by Alastair Reid (London: Cape Goliard Press, 1967; New York: Grossman, 1968); *Twenty Love Poems and a Song of Despair*, translated by W. S. Merwin (London: Jonathan Cape, 1969); *A New Decade: Poems, 1958-1967*, translated by Ben Belitt and Alastair Reid (New York: Grove, 1969); *Pablo Neruda: The Early Poems*, translated by David Ossman and Carlos B. Hagen (Minneapolis: New Rivers Press, 1969); *Selected Poems*, translated by Anthony Kerrigan and others (London: Jonathan Cape, 1970; New York: Delacorte Press, 1972); *The Captain's Verses*, translated by Donald D. Walsh (New York: New Directions, 1972); *Extravagaria*, translated by Alastair Reid (Jonathan Cape, 1972; New York: Farrar Straus, & Giroux, 1974); *New Poems, 1968-1970*, translated by Ben Belitt (New York: Grove Press, 1972); *Residence on Earth*, translated by Donald D. Walsh (New York: New Directions, 1973); *Five Decades: A Selection (Poems 1925-1970)*, edited and translated by Ben Belitt (New York: Grove Press, 1974); *Fully Empowered: Plenos poderes*, translated by Alastair Reid (New York: Farrar, Straus, & Giroux, 1975); *Isla Negra: A Notebook*, translated by Alastair Reid (New York: Farrar, Straus, & Giroux, 1980); *The Separate Rose*, translated by William O'Daly (Port Townsend, Washington: Copper Canyon Press, 1985); *100 Love Sonnets*, trans. by Stephen J. Tapscott (Austin: University of Texas Press, 1986); *Winter Garden*, translated by William O'Daly (Port Townsend, Washington: Copper Canyon Press, 1986); *Stones of Chile*, translated by Dennis Maloney (Fredonia, NY: White Pine Press, 1987); *Stones of Sky*, translated by James Nolan (Port Townsend, Washington: Copper Canyon Press, 1987); *The Sea and the Bells*, translated by William O'Daly (Port Townsend, Washington: Copper Canyon Press, 1988); *The House at Isla Negra*, translated by Dennis Maloney and Clark Zlotchew (Fredonia, New York: White Pine Press, 1988); *Late and Posthumous Poems, 1968-1974*, edited and translated by Ben Belitt (New York: Grove Press, 1989); *The Book of Questions*, translated by William O'Daly (Port Townsend: Copper Canyon Press, 1991); *Neruda's Garden: An Anthology of Odes*, translated by Maria Jacketti (Pittsburgh: Latin American Literary Review Press, 1995); *Ceremonial Songs*, translated by Maria Jacketti (Pittsburgh: Latin American Literary Review Press, 1996).

Dead Gallop

Like ashes, like seas peopling themselves,
in the submerged slowness, in the shapelessness,
or as one hears from the crest of the roads
the crossed bells crossing,
having that sound now sundered from the metal,
confused, ponderous, turning to dust
in the very milling of the too distant forms,
either remembered or not seen,
and the perfume of the plums that rolling on the ground
rot in time, infinitely green.

All that so swift, so living,
yet motionless, like the pulley wild within itself,
those motor wheels in short.
Existing like the dry stitches in the tree's seams,
silent, all around, in such a way,
all the limbs mixing their tails.
But from where, through where, on what shore?
The constant, uncertain surrounding, so silent,
like the lilacs around the convent
or death's coming to the tongue of the ox
that stumbles to the ground, guard down, with horns that
    struggle to blow.

Therefore, in the stillness, stopping, to perceive,
then, like an immense fluttering, above,
like dead bees or numbers,
ah, what my pale heart cannot embrace,
in multitudes, in tears scarcely shed,
and human efforts, anguish,
black deeds suddenly discovered
like ice, vast disorder,
oceanic, to me who enter singing,
as if with a sword among the defenseless.

Well now, what is it made of, that upsurge of doves
that exists between night and time, like a moist ravine?
That sound so prolonged now
that falls lining the roads with stones,
or rather, when only an hour
grows suddenly, stretching without pause.

Within the ring of summer
the great calabash trees once listen,
stretching out their pity-laden plants,
it is made of that, of what with much wooing,
of the fullness, dark with heavy drops.

—Translated from the Spanish by Donald D. Walsh

(from *Residencia en la tierra 1*, 1933)

Dream Horse

Unnecessary, seeing myself in mirrors,
with a fondness for weeks, biographers, papers,
I tear from my heart the captain of hell,
I establish clauses indefinitely sad.

I wander from one point to another, I absorb illusions,
I converse with tailorbirds in their nests:
they, frequently, with cold and fatal voices
sing and put to flight the maledictions.

There is an extensive country in the sky
with the superstitious carpets of the rainbow
and with vesperal vegetation;
toward there I journey, not without a certain fatigue,
treading an earth disturbed by rather fresh tombs,
I dream among those plants of tangled vegetation.

I pass among used papers, among origins,
dressed like an original and dejected being:
I love the wasted honey of respect,
the gentle catechism among whose leaves
sleep aged, faded violets,
and the brooms, pathetically eager to assist,
in their appearance there are, no doubt, sorrow and certainty.
I destroy the whistling rose and the ravishing worry:
I break beloved extremes; and even more,
I await uniform, measureless time:
a taste that I have in my heart depresses me.

What a day has arrived! What a thick light of milk,
compact, digital, indulges me!
I have heard its red horse neigh
naked, shoeless and radiant.
I cross with it over the churches,
I gallop through barracks stripped of soldiers
and a foul army pursues me.
Its eucalyptus eyes steal the shadows,
its bell body gallops and strikes.

I need a lightningstroke of persistent splendor,
a festive relative to take on my inheritance.

—*Translated from the Spanish by Donald D. Walsh*

(from *Residencia en la tierra I*, 1933)

Ritual of My Legs

For a long time I have stayed looking at my long legs,
with infinite and curious tenderness, with my accustomed passion,
as if they had been the legs of a divine woman,
deeply sunk in the abyss of my thorax:
and, to tell the truth, when time, when time passes
over the earth, over the roof, over my impure head,
and it passes, time passes, and in my bed I do not feel at night
    that a woman is breathing sleeping naked and at my side,
then strange, dark things take the place of the absent one,
vicious, melancholy thoughts
sow heavy possibilities in my bedroom,
and so, then, I look at my legs as if they belonged to another body
and were stuck strongly and gently to my insides.

Like stems or feminine adorable things,
from the knees they rise, cylindrical and thick,
with a disturbed and compact material of existence:
like brutal, thick goddess arms,
like trees monstrously dressed as human beings,
like fatal, immense lips thirsty and tranquil,
they are, there, the best part of my body:
the entirely substantial part, without complicated content
of senses or tracheas or intestines or ganglia:

nothing but the pure, the sweet, and the thick part of my own life,
nothing but form and volume existing,
guarding life, nevertheless, in a complete way.

People cross through the world nowadays
scarcely remembering that they possess a body and life within it,
and there is fear, in the world there is fear of the words that designate the body,
and one talks favorably of clothes,
it is possible to speak of trousers, of suits,
and of women's underwear (of "ladies'" stockings and garters)
as if the articles and the suits went completely empty through the streets
and a dark and obscene clothes closet occupied the world.

Suits have existence, color, form, design,
and a profound place in our myths, too much of a place,
there is too much furniture and there are too many rooms in the world
and my body lives downcast among and beneath so many things,
with an obsession of slavery and chains.

Well, my knees, like knots,
private, functional, evident,
separate neatly the halves of my legs:
and really two different worlds, two different sexes
are not so different as the two halves of my legs.

From the knee to the foot a hard form,
mineral, coldly useful, appears,
a creature of bone and persistence,
and the ankles are now nothing but the naked purpose,
exactitude and necessity definitively disposed.

Without sensuality, short and hard, and masculine,
my legs exist, there, and endowed
with muscular groups like complementary animals,
and there too a life, a solid, subtle, sharp life
endures without trembling, waiting and performing.

At my feet ticklish
and hard like the sun, and open like flowers,
and perpetual, magnificent soldiers
in the gray war of space,
everything ends, life definitvely ends at my feet,
what is foreign and hostile begins there:

the names of the world, the frontier and the remote,
the substantive and the adjectival too great for my heart
originate there with dense and cold constancy.

Always,
manufactured products, socks, shoes,
or simply infinite air,
there will be between my feet and the earth
stressing the isolated and solitary part of my being,
something tenaciously involved between my life and the earth,
something openly unconquerable and unfriendly.

—*Translated from the Spanish by Donald D. Walsh*

(from *Residencia en la tierra I*, 1933)

The Southern Ocean

Of emaciated salt and imperiled throat
are made the roses of the solitary sea,
the water broken nonetheless,
and fearful birds,
and there is only night accompanied
by day, and day accompanied
by a shelter, by a
hoof, by silence.

In the silence the wind grows
with its single leaf and its battered flower,
and the sand that has only touch and silence,
it is nothing, it is a shadow,
the tread of a wandering horse,
it is nothing but a wave that time has received,
because all the waters go to the cold eyes
of time that watches beneath the ocean.

Its eyes have already died of dead water and doves,
and they are two holes of bitter breadth
through which enter fish with blood-stained teeth
and whales seeking emeralds,
and skeletons of pale horsemen undone
by the slow jellyfish, and besides

various societies of poisonous myrtle,
isolated hands, arrows,
scaly revolvers,
interminably run along its cheeks
and devour its eyes of dismissed salt.

When the moon delivers up its shipwrecks,
its boxes, its dead
covered with male poppies,
when into the moon sack fall
the suits buried in the sea
with their long torments, their demolished beards,
their heads that water and pride sought forever,
in the expanse knees are heard falling
toward the bottom of the sea, knees brought by the moon
in its stone sack worn away by tears
and by the bites of sinister fish.

It is true, it is the moon descending
with cruel sponge shakes, it is, nonetheless,
the moon staggering among the lairs,
the moon gnawed by the water's shouts,
the bellies of the moon, its scales
of discharged steel: and from then on
at the end of the Ocean it descends,
blue and blue, pierced by blues,
blind blues of blind substance,
dragging its corrupted cargo,
divers, planks, fingers,
fisher of the blood that at the peaks of the sea
has been split by great misfortunes.

But I speak of a shore, it is there that the sea
lashes with fury and the waves smash
the ashen walls. What is this? Is it a shadow?
It is not the shadow, it is the sand of the sad republic,
it is an arrangement of seaweed, there are wings, there is
a pecking at the breast of heaven:
oh surface wounded by the waves,
oh fountain of the sea,
if the rain assures your secrets, if the interminable wind
kills the birds, if only the sky,
I want only to bite your coasts and die,

I want only to look at the mouths of the stones
through which the secrets emerge covered with foam.

It is a solitary region, I have already spoken
of this so solitary region,
where the earth is covered with ocean,
and there is no one but some hoofprints,
there is no one but the wind, there is no one
but the rain that falls upon the waters of the sea,
no one but the rain that grows upon the sea.

—Translated from the Spanish by Donald D. Walsh

(from *Residencia en la tierra ii*, 1935)

Melancholy in the Families

I keep a blue flask,
inside it an ear and a portrait:
when night forces
the owl's feathers,
when the raucous cherry tree
shatters its lips and threatens
with husks that the ocean wind often penetrates,
I know that there are great sunken expanses,
quartz in ingots,
slime,
blue waters for a battle,
much silence, many
veins of retreats and camphors,
fallen things, medals, acts of tenderness,
parachutes, kisses.

It is only the passage from one day toward another,
a single bottle moving across the seas,
and a dining room to which come roses,
a dining room abandoned
like a thorn: I refer
to a shattered goblet, to a curtain, to the depths
of a deserted room through which a river flows
dragging the stones. It is a house
set on the foundations of the rain,

a two-storied house with compulsory windows
and strictly faithful climbing vines.

I go in the evening, I arrive
covered with mud and death,
dragging the earth and its roots,
and its vague belly where corpses
sleep with wheat,
metals, overturned elephants.

But on top of everything there is a terrible,
a terrible abandoned dining room,
with broken jugs
and vinegar flowing under the chairs,
a rather dark lightningbolt
stopped from the moon, and I look for
a comparison within myself:
perhaps it is a tent surrounded by the sea
and torn clothes oozing brine.
It is only an abandoned dining room,
and around it there are expanses,
submerged factories, boards
that only I know,
because I am sad and old,
and I know the earth, and I am sad.

—*Translated from the Spanish by Donald D. Walsh*

(from *Residencia en la tierra II*, 1935)

Ode to Sadness

Sadness, beetle
with seven shattered feet,
egg in a spider's web,
wounded rat,
bitch's skeleton.
Don't come in here.
Don't advance.
Get away from here.
Return to the South

with your umbrella;
return to the North
with your serpent fangs.
A poet lives here.
Sadness cannot penetrate
these doors.
Through these windows
the world's air enters,
pure red roses,
flags embroidered
with souls and their victories.
You cannot—
don't come in here.
Rumble
your bat-wings.
With my feet, I'll crush
the feathers falling from your cloak.
I'll sweep the remains
of your cadaver
and sent it into the wind's four corners.
I'll wring your neck.
I'll sew up your eyes.
I'll cut your shroud
and bury your biting bones
under an apple tree's springtime.

—*Translated from the Spanish by Maria Jacketti*

(from *Nuevas odas elementales*, 1956)

PERMISSIONS

"Dead Gallop," "Dream Horse," "Ritual of My Legs," "The Southern Ocean," and "Melancholy in the Families,"
Reprinted from *Residence on Earth*, trans. by Donald D. Walsh (New York: New Directions, 1973). Copyright ©by Pablo Neruda and Donald D. Walsh; ©1973 by New Directions Publishing Corporation. Reprinted by permission of New Directions Publishing Corporation.

"Ode to Sadness"
Reprinted from *Neruda's Garden: An Anthology of Odes*, trans. and selected by Maria Jacketti (Pittsburgh: Latin American Literary Review Press, 1995). Translation copyright ©1995 by Latin American Literary Review Press. Reprinted by permission of Latin American Literary Review Press.

Cees Nooteboom [The Netherlands]
1933

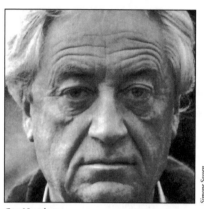

Cees Nooteboom

Simone Sassen

Born in The Hague in 1933, Cees Nooteboom was educated in monastery schools in the southern part of The Netherlands. He now lives in Amsterdam, but spends much of the year in Spain and in travel, recently in Australia and Japan.

Although perhaps better known as a novelist and travel writer, poetry is at the core of Nooteboom's oeuvre. His first book, *De doden zoeken een huis* (1956), contains many of the themes he was to explore throughout his prolific career, including issues relating to time and death. Over the years—despite a pause in his poetic writing from 1964 to 1978—his poetry has grown stronger and more complex. The publication of his collected poetry, *Vuurtijd, ijstijd: Gedichten, 1955–1983* in 1984, revealed a poet of intensely sober observation. His first English language collection, *The Captain of the Butterflies*, was published by Sun & Moon Press in 1997.

Nooteboom is recognized throughout the world for his many novels, including *Philip en de anderen* (1955), *Rituelen* (1980, *Rituals, 1983*)—for which he won the Mobil Oil Pegasus Prize—*In Nederland* (1984, *In the Dutch Mountains,* 1987)—which was awarded the Multatuli Prize—and, more recently, *Het Volgende Verhaal* (1991, *The Following Story,* 1994). Among his travel writings are *Een avond in Isfahan* (1978; an evening in Isfahan) and *Berlijnse notities* (1990, notes of Berlin), and, more recently, *Roads to Santiago*, published in English in 2000.

BOOKS OF POETRY:

De doden zoeben een huis (Amsterdam: Querido, 1956); *Koude gedichten* (Amsterdam: Querido, 1959); *Het zwarte gedicht* (Amsterdam: Querido, 1960); *Gesloten gedichten* (Amsterdam: De Bezige Bij, 1964); *Aanwezig, Atwezig* (Amsterdam: Arbeiderspers, 1970); *Open als een schelp, dicht als een steen: Gedichten* (Amsterdam: Arbeiderspers, 1978); *Aas: Gedichten* (Amsterdam: Arbeiderspers, 1982); *Vuurtijd, ijstijd: Gedichtedn, 1955-1983* (Amsterdam: Arbeiderspers, 1984); *Zo kon het zijn* (Amsterdam: Atlas, 1999).

ENGLISH LANGUAGE TRANSLATIONS:

The Captain of the Butterflies, translated by Leonard Nathan and Herlinde Spahr (Los Angeles: Sun & Moon Press, 1997)

The Sealed Riders

Hole in the dark
they named the light of moon
and with their hands disfigured by it
they wanted its measure

and became a new movement
an army of rags with veiled faces
hidden in crowns and coats
on horses of human flesh.

They did not bear names
other than their own
some years they are invisible
eyes mouths ears all sealed

there'll be no end to this procession

I see them, see them
and burn.

—*Translated from the Dutch by Leonard Nathan and Herlinde Spahr*

(from *Aanwezig, Atwizig,* 1970)

Abschied

Not for someone else
this foolishness,
but for you.

When the high-rise is gone, when this is a plain,
and you a statue, self-raised,
and I touch you,

When all things suffer like me,
nailed down with sorrow, when to know nothing
is to sneak like a fungus through tissue

you stand still, silvered, splattered, the eastwind vagrant
around you, and around me,
I made a disaster out of the ordinary.

I'll forget everything about you, except you.
You rage through the space I occupy,
your love is fate.

Through your likeness I see the longing
from which we were expelled. I had offered everything,
you had refused everything. You had offered everything,
I did not see it.
Quiet now.

Death is a male disease.
You go around and gather up life.
Now quiet.

— *Translated from the Dutch by Leonard Nathan and Herlinde Spahr*

(from *Aas,* 1982)

Grail

Remember the time
that we were searching for something,
something quite precise,
a concept, paraphrase, definition,
a theme, thesis, supposition,
a summa of what we did not know,
something we wished
to assume or measure or tally
between all things obscure?

You know, don't you know
how we always wandered off, dividing
the concept and the quest,
Augustine the brothels, Albert the numbers,
Jorge the mirrors, Immanuel home, Pablo the forms,
Wolfgang the colors,
Teresa, Blaise, Friedrich, Leonardo, Augustus,
always tallying and measuring between words and notes, thinking
among nuns, soldiers and poets,

breaking, looking, splitting,
till the bones, the shadow,
a glimmer, a narrowing down
in senses or images,
until in a glass or a number
but always so briefly
a hiccup of a thought, of a way,
so endlessly vague became visible?

—*Translated from the Dutch by Leonard Nathan and Herlinde Spahr*

(from *Aas*, 1982)

Cartography
for Cristina Barroso

I

Only the bird sees what I see,
the impassable ways in my hand,
a golden and ash-colored beauty,
the surprising accident
of a world drawn only once,
a though construed of matter,
a painting missing its painter,
my secret universe.

Oceans, steppes, volcanoes, the humming
of their names from always younger mouths.
My making hand follows their forms,
vein, chasm, slope, ravine,
the hidden lines of strata and ore,
diary of desert, of wilderness, of mirroring sea,
that which I am.

II

Ice age, star time,
my past exists in locked-up images,
called out by fire and water,
a registry of resin and sand.

That is how I show myself,
how I hide myself,
in ciphers of height and depth,
layers of color
on an atlas as big as the world.

III

Measure, says the book of maps.
Measure, given.
Measure, real
But given by whom?
Real for whom?

The tiny plane hovering above the shoreline,
shadow of Phoenician sails,
constellations, plumb line, calipers, ink,
the slow page from Strabo,
the prows of Aeneas, Odysseus,
or how the sea changes to paper,
the waves into words,
the exacting task of shrinking,
the art of meter and time.

IV

The inner spectacle
piles question upon question.
Were the dogs visible on that spit of land?

The death of the flies, poison of the flowers,
the track of the enemy,
the surveyor in his hotel?
Who followed the train with the future dead,
measured the slowness of the way?
Fate is not set down on maps.
Fate is all ours.

Grids, shading, scale, the constraint
of coordinates, words of magic
for the world as a thing.

But I go with my living earth
of rivers and marshes, bends and willows,
which I compose in my image.
When I retrace them I leave my seal,
a map painted
of soul.

—*Translated from the Dutch by Leonard Nathan and Herlinde Spahr*

(from *Zo kon het zijn*, 1999)

Mail

But then, are your ideas so clear
the mailman asked. Just at that moment
the sky darkened,
but that was another matter,
things around here happen that way,
from one moment to the next.

That means rain, he said, and it did.
Big drops. Behind him I could see the bay,
a plane leaden in the clouds,
slow. It landed.

Where do such seconds go?
How much rustling can be missed?
Which conversations cannot be
pulverized against the time-wall, in a lapse
of memory, somewhere at the bottom
of a dream?

Fiction, a house on a hill,
the psalm of rain, page six,
maillman, descent, downward path
into oblivion,
his, mine,
that fat of time
as someone might turn a page
without having read,

all written
for nothing.

—Translated from the Dutch by Leonard Nathan and Herlinde Spahr

(from *Zo kon ket zijn*, 1999)

Harbalorifa

So many forms of existence! So many creatures
to suffer and laugh in these stony hills!

The figtree is bent toward the south,
above us the soft snoring of a plane.

My friend is waiting near a bush with sharp thorns.
He knows the story of his fate,

we see the glitter of the sea
among gallnuts and thistles, a sail in the distance.

Everything sleeps. Give me some other life and I won't take it.
Shells and crickets, my cup is full of eternal noon.

The stream I drank from yesterday was cool and clear.
I saw the laurel tree's reflection. I saw the shadow

of the leaves drift away across the bottom.
This was all I ever wanted. Harbalorifa!

My age hangs on a thread. So I am the spider
above the path, weaving its polygonal time

—Translated from the Dutch by Leonard Nathan and Herlinde Spahr

(from *Zo kon het zijn*, 1999)

PERMISSIONS

"Mail," "Harbalorifa," "The Sealed Riders," "Abschied," "Cartography," and "Grail"
Reprinted from *The Captain of the Butterflies*, trans. by Leonard Nathan and Herlinde Spahr (Los Angeles:
Sun & Moon Press, 1997). English language translation ©1997 by Leonard Nathan and Herlinde Spahr.
Reprinted by permission of Sun & Moon Press.

János Pilinszky [Hungary]
1921–1981

János Pilinszky was born and educated in Budapest, first studying law and then philosophy. His earliest poems appeared in literary reviews of 1940. He was drafted into the Hungarian army toward the end of the war, and was evacuated to Germany, making his way back to Hungary in 1945.

János Pilinszky

After various editorial jobs, Pilinszky became a staff member of the Catholic weekly, *Új Ember*, where he remained until his death. His first slim collection of poetry, *Harmadnapon* (On the Third Day) established his reputation, and characterized his poetic stance as an existential Catholic concerned with human suffering. After this he traveled widely, spending long periods in France and visiting England several times. His collected poems, *Kráter (Crater)* were published in 1976. In 1980 he was awarded the Kossuth Prize.

BOOKS OF POETRY:

Trapéz és korlát. Versek (Budapest: Ezüstkor, 1946); *Aranymadár. Verses mesék* (Budapest: Magvetö, 1957); *Harmadnapon* (Budapest: Szépirodalmi, 1959); *Rekviem. Versek és próza* (Budapest:Magvetö, 1964); *Nagyvárosi ikonok. Összegyüjtött versek 1940-1970* (Budapest: Szépirodalmi, 1970); *Szálkák* (Budapest: Szépirodalmi, 1972); *Végkifejlet. Versek és színmüvek* (Budapest: Szépirodalmi, 1974); *A nap születése. Régi és új verses mesék* (Budapest: Móra, 1974); *Kráter. Összegyüjtött és új versek* (Budapest: Szépirodalmi, 1976); *Válogatott versek* (Budapest: Magvetö and Szépirodalmi, 1978); *Összegyüjtött versei* (Budapest: Szépirodalmi, 1987).

ENGLISH LANGUAGE TRANSLATIONS:

Selected Poems, trans. by Ted Hughes and János Csokits (Manchester: Carcanet New Press, 1976); *Crater: Poems 1974-75*, trans. by Peter Jay (London: Anvil Press Poetry, 1978); *Scaffold in Winter: Selected Poems*, trans. by I. L. Halasz de Beky (Toronto: Box Humana, 1982); *The Desert of Love* [expanded edition of *Selected Poems*] (London: Anvil Press Poetry, 1989); *Metropolitan Icons: Selected Poems of János Pilinszky in Hungarian and English*, trans. by Emery George (Lampeter, Dyfed, Wales: The Edwin Mellen Press, 1995).

Fable

Once upon a time
there was a lonely wolf
lonelier than the angels.

He happened to come to a village.
He fell in love with the first house he saw.

Already he loved its walls
the caresses of its bricklayers.
But the window stopped him.

In the room sat people.
Apart from God nobody ever
found them so beautiful
as this child-like beast.

So at night he went into the house.
He stopped in the middle of the room
and never moved from there any more.

He stood all through the night, with wide eyes
and so into the morning when he was beaten to death.

—Translated from the Hungarian by Ted Hughes and János Csokits

(from *Nagyvárosi ikonok*, 1970)

Epilogue
to Pierre Emmanuel

Remember? On the faces.
Remember? The empty ditch.
Remember? It's streaming down.
Remember? I stand in the sun.

You read the Paris Journal.
Since then, winter has come. Winter's night.
You lay the table beside me.
You make the bed in the moonlight.

Catching your breath, you undress
in the dark of the bare house.
You let down your skirt, and take off your blouse.
Your back is a bare tombstone.

Image of wretched strength.
Is anybody here?
                    A waking dream:
unanswered, I cross
the rooms lying in the depths of mirrors.

Is this my face? This face?
The light, the silence, and the judgment are shattered
as this stone, my face, hurtles towards me
out of the snow-white mirror!

And the horsemen! The horsemen!
Darkness oppresses me. The lamplight hurts me.
A slack thread of water plays
on the motionless china.

I rattle at the closed doors.
Your room is dark as a shaft.
The walls glare with cold.
I smudge my weeping on the wall.

You snow-heaped house-tops, help me!
Now it is night. Now let every orphaned thing
shine out, before there arises
the sun of nothingness. And you, in vain,
shine! I lean my head to the wall.
From all around me the dead city
holds towards me, mercy towards the dead,
a handful of snow.

I loved you! A shout. A sigh.
A cloud in flight.
And through the slush, under breaking dawn,
at a heavy torrential trot, come the horsemen.

—*Translated from the Hungarian by Ted Hughes and János Csokits*

(from *Nagyvárosi ikonok*, 1970)

Enough

Creation, no matter how vast,
is more cramped than a roost.
From here to there. Stone, tree, house.
I potter about, come early, come too late.

Yet, now and again, some person enters
and in a moment everything has opened—
the sight of a face, a presence is enough,
and the wallpaper starts to bleed.

Enough, yes, enough a hand
as it stirs a cup of coffee
or as it "withdraws from the introduction"
and enough
that we forget the place
the airless row of windows, yes,
that returning, at night, to our room
we accept the unacceptable.

—Translated from the Hungarian by Ted Hughes and János Csokits

(from *Szálkák*, 1972)

Crater

We've met. We go on meeting.
In a cigar store. At an auction.
You were rummaging for something. You're dislodging
something. I'd like to flee. I'm staying.
I light up a cigarette. You're leaving.

You get off and get on.
I get on and get off.
Cigarette. You're pacing. I'm pacing.
We walk in the same spot; like a murderer,
I tailgate you as you walk.

It's bird-twitter, the way
you reproach me for my birth.
For our standing here. Then, in the cul-de-sac

of a leg of the journey, my mutter
starts in rolling, pearls off your enormous
limbs and off that triumphant
and blinding something
that is not you any more.

Your snub, this licentious
whisk, written in stone, has touched me
so that my glance—two pebbles—has
just been rolling and rolling since
in a snow-white crater. My two eyes,
two eyes sputter: my salvation.

—Translated from the Hungarian by Peter Jay

(from *Kráter*, 1976)

Henrikas Radauskas [Lithuania/U S A]
1910–1970

Born in 1910, Henrikas Radauskas spent his child-
hood in a village near Panevėžys in the north-cen-
tral part of Lithuania. His family moved to Siberia
at the beginning of World War I, and it was there he
attended elementary school. In 1921 he returned to
Lithuania, graduating from Panevėžys high school,
and, in 1929, graduated from the Teachers Institute
there. For a short period of time he taught school,
and then entered the University of Kaunas. After
completing his studies, he became a radio announcer
in the city of Klaip—da and a copy editor in Kaunas.
In 1937 he assumed the editorship of the publica-
tions division of the Lithuanian Ministry of Educa-
tion.

Henrikas Radauskas

In 1944, Radauskas, like many other Lithuanians
before him, attempted to emigrate to the Soviet Union; but he and his wife were caught between
the retreating Nazis and the advancing Red Army, and were forced to settle in Germany, first in
Berlin and later in Reutlingen by the French and Swiss borders. In 1949 they emigrated to the
United States, spending a year in Baltimore before settling in Chicago.

American life was difficult for the couple, and he labored for ten years as a machine operator
for a company that produced chairs before being able to secure a job as a translator and copy
editor at the Library of Congress in Washington, D.C.—a job he held until his death in 1970.

Radauskas published only four books of poetry, but they were of sufficient merit to establish
him as a major Lithuanian poet in an artistic scene of great sophistication. Other major
Lithuanian poets, both émigrés and those writing in Lithuania, wrote poetry grounded in tradi-
tional German and Lithuanian conventions; but, as Radauskas's translator has written,
"Radauskas sought to shape the things of the world as he saw them into a personal universe, a
controlled place which the terrors of history...could be mitigated and overcome."

The result is a poetry that at times seems highly influenced by surrealism, but is, nonethe-
less, highly idiosyncratic, closer to a vision of the naïve artist who compresses images and time
to create a work of stunning originality.

BOOKS OF POETRY:
Fontanas (1935); *Strėlė danguje* (1950); *Žiemos daina* (1955); *Žaibai ir vėjai* (1965).

ENGLISH LANGUAGE TRANSLATIONS:

Chimeras in the Tower: Selected Poems of Henrikas Radauskas, translated by Jonas Zdanys
(Middletown, Connecticut: Wesleyan University Press, 1986)

Sunday

In a room dead for twenty years
An old woman's shadow yawns, turns an empty
Coffee grinder, the clock shows Sundy,
The cuckoo quieted, stabbed a guest in the inn.

A sleeping woman reads a scorched book:
The Terrible History of the Demon Belphegor.
In her palms are Saturn's broken lines.
The double walls are filled with ducats and bones.

An anemic voice runs up the cellar stairs,
Coloratura dripping candles and tears.
The wall rips, the rubber girl falls,
Violins carry the bloody heart to the garden.

A giant laughing maple knocks at the ruddy
Coffin decorated with flutes and fioritura.
Poveri fiori. Poisoned violets faint.
The shadow of the voice runs to the vanished house.

—Translated from the Lithuanian by Jonas Zdanys

Harbor

Locked up in a midday hard as diamond
My eyes begin to fail.
The shore is charged with a fierce light:
A holiday of nails, broken glass, daggers—
Who will give me a helping hand?

And steamer and locomotive
Sirens carve the rippled air,
And crabs and lobsters crawl
Between fishermen's stone hands,
And a crowd of screaming blacks
Pierces me like knives.

The shore is charged with a hot light.
Who will cover the fire with clouds,
Help me to wait for the cold night?
A holiday of lightning, flames, embers.

And the ocean rocks with boats
And glitters with crooked mirrors.

—Translated from the Lithuanian by Jonas Zdanys

Madonna and Fly

Beyond her shoulders—a moon river falling golden from heaven near which curly-headed trees run from the hills like a herd of green sheep and in which a miniature horseman waters a steed the size of a grasshopper.

Opening a purple robe blossoming with pearls and sapphires, she gives the yellow babe a round red breast which he indifferently sucks while staring grimly at a fly crawling on the marble balustrade.

"O that man's mind, that his heart could understand her painfully mystical smile!"— wrote von Bock. (The child's fingers, which pinch his mother's flesh like pliers, are hidden by his right shoulder.)

In the middle of the night, after the lone light on the ceiling has squeaked and burned out, the madonna steps out of the frame, passes by the drunken Rubens and the savage Goya, walks down the stairs to the cellar and puts the child into a polished Assyrian black basalt bathtub. Feeling the stone's cold, he begins to cry, but in front of her the complying door has begun to open, and she, accompanied by the buzzing fly, walks out into the neon-lighted swimming, melting, disappearing street.

—Translated from the Lithuanian by Jonas Zdanys

Ball

It is already after midnight, the ball having reached a hysterical climax, as lovers begin to finger the hair of their squealing ladies, and couples, overcoming the indifferent laws of physics, rise in sudden curves, and memory no longer listens to you and you no longer remember what you had to remember, and the hands and feet of dancers swim willy-nilly in the gentle and transparent fog, chandeliers on the ceiling stretch and turn into swirling spirals of light which break into sharp edges—the room begins to shout, outscreaming the tearing orchestra's black lightning rumble, and it becomes totally dark, and you remember the dead soldier's violet face (the fighting was still on then in West Berlin)—and the wind rocks the only light in the whole cosmos and blows into your eyes a light rain and the dryly rustling leaves of an invisible tree.

—Translated from the Lithuanian by Jonas Zdanys

In the Hospital Garden

Through the hospital window chloroform
Flows from a broken bottle
Into evening's garden,
And a poplar's feet fall asleep
And its hands get lost in dreams.

And goblets of wild rose buds
Chase air like fish—
A bush winces and staggers,
Grabs with its branches at a low
Cloud, and collapses.

And the nightingale can't
Count to three:
The melody melts on the third trill,
Falls into a yellow pond,
And suddenly the whole garden brightens:

I burn like a funeral candle
Near my hanging coffin
And swim into the bottomless box.
And the weathervane in the tower
Tosses terrified and squeaks prayers

—Translated from the Lithuanian by Jonas Zdanys

Apollo

His profile is as painful and thin
As the blade of a sword. Not long ago
Apollo walked by here,
And the glass echo of his lyre

Will remain forever
In these frightened rooms,
And his cold marble face
In this cruel night, and I have
To sing the tired, old
Songs of people who have died.

Quick swallows crisscross the sky,
Jubilant flutes dance in the woods,
And the sun paints the ringing landscape
Red as a painted woman,
And I have to sing the old
Songs of people who have died.

—Translated from the Lithuanian by Jonas Zdanys

Conversations of Dogs

Through darkening telegraph poles
At the crossroads, near grey piles of gravel,
I see frail farmsteads scattered
Against the dimmed autumn background.

Beyond the highway, beyond the falling birches,
A shepherd's voice in the marsh throbs among ferns.
Rain drips slowly
From horses's manes.

In the woods woodpecker knocks don't knock.
Evening fell beyond the clouds.
Things died out.
It's dark.

Who threw me into this darkness?
I walk splashing invisible puddles.
Somewhere far off, beyond the horizon,
Conversations of dogs.

—Translated from the Lithuanian by Jonas Zdanys

Ophelia

When I was a child
I did not want to learn to swim.
I cried,
Bit my nurse's hand.

When the prince pushed me away,
I dived,
Wouldn't have come up,
But now—
I float on my back
Between the clouds and grass,
Sing out of boredom.

The morning's cold.
The stone philosopher said:
The universe is cooling,
The cold will kill God.

Singing at night
I floated by a gypsy fire.
They ran to the river
Dancing,
Picked up the melody,
Added a chorus.

The current's strong.
I'll never reach the bank.
I can already hear the sea.

I hope my teacher was right:
That earth is really round.
And in several years,
Adorned with crystals of salt,
I'll return by water to Elsinore.

If the gypsies were telling the truth,
That the prince died poisoned,
I'll forget I can swim
And jump into the river.

—*Translated from the Lithuanian by Jonas Zdanys*

PERMISSIONS

"Sunday," "Harbor," "Madonna and Fly," "Ball," "In the Hospital Garden," "Apollo," "Conversations of Dogs," and "Ophelia"
Reprinted from *Chimeras in the Tower,* trans. by Jonas Zdanys (Hanover, New Hampshire: University Press of New England [Wesleyan University Press], 1986. Copyright ©1986 by Jonas Zdanys. Reprinted by permission of the University Press of New England.

Míltos Sahtoúris   [Greece]
1919

Born in Athens on July 29, 1919, Míltos Sahtoúris regards his place of origin as Hýdra, the home of his great, great grandfather who was an admiral in the Greek War of Independence. Sahtoúris' father was a State legal consul, and his job soon necessitated the family's move to Thessaoníki, and later to Náfplion and back to Athens when the poet was five. But during the summer Sahtoúris was sent to the family estate in Pelopponesos, opposite Hýdra, where he fished and hunted in the woodside. As a youth he attended the University of Athens, studying law, but upon his father's death in 1939, left the university without a degree and burned his books.

As a student he had despised Greek literature, particularly poetry (with exception of Caváfis and Kariotákis). But during his first few years in the university, he published a small volume of verse, *The Music of the Islands* under the pseudonym Míltos Hrisánthis, but which he later rejected as juvenalia. In 1944, however, he became compelled again to write. But this time his work was influenced by Greek surrealism, represented particularly in the poetry of Níkos Engonópoulos and Andréas Emberícos, and the early work of Odysseus Elýtis. Writing to translator Kimon Friar, he wrote "Surrealism freed me from many things. It freed me, first of all, from an austere paternal education and from a narrow family tradition. As a technique, it taught me to listen to what's genuine in poetry and to use all words fearlessly."

Over the next decades, often living a hermetic and poverty-striken life, Sahtoúris produced many books of poetry, including *The Forgotten Woman* (1945), *Ballads* (1948), *The Face to the Wall* (1952), *When I Speak to You* (1956), *The Phantoms or Joy in the Other Street* (1958), *The Stroll* (1960), *The Stigmata* (1962), *The Seal or the Eighth Moon* (1964), *The Vessel* (1971), *Poems, 1945– 1971*, and *Color Wounds* (1980). In 1962 he was awarded the Second State Prize in Greece for poetry, and he shared the Third State Prize in 1964. In 1972 he received a Ford Foundation Grant.

BOOKS OF POETRY:

The Forgotten Woman (1945); *Ballads* (1948); *With Face to the Wall* (1952); *When I Speak to You* (1956); *The Phantoms or Joy in the Other Street* (1958); *The Stroll* (1960); *The Stigmata* (1962); *The Seal or The Eighth Moon* (1964); *The Vessel* (1971); *Poems, 1945-1971* (1971); *Color Wounds* (1980).

POETRY IN ENGLISH

Selected Poems, trans. from the Greek by Kimon Friar (Old Chatham, New York: Sachem Press, 1982).

The Difficult Sunday

Since morning I've been looking upward at a better bird
since morning I've been rejoicing at a snake coiled around my neck

Broken water glasses on the rug
crimson flowers the cheeks of the prophetess
when she lifts the dress of fate
something will grow out of this joy
a new tree without flowers
or an innocent new eyelash
or an adored word
that has not kissed forgetfulness on the mouth

Outside the bells are clamoring
outside unimaginable friends are waiting for me
they lift a dawn high and twirl it round
what weariness what weariness
yellow dress—an eagle embroidered—
green parrot—I close my eyes—it shrieks
always always always
the orchestra plays counterfeit tunes
what suffering eyes what women
what loves what voices what loves
friend love blood friend
friend give me your hand what cold

It was freezing
I no longer know the hour when they all died
and I remained with an amputated friend
and with a blooded branch for company

—*Translated from the Greek by Kimon Friar*

(from *The Forgotten Woman*, 1945)

Beauty

He sprinkled ugliness with beauty
he took a guitar
and walked along a riverbank
singing

He lost his voice
the delirious lady stole it
who cut off her head in the crimson waters
and the poor man no longer has a voice to sing with
and the river rolls
the tranquil head with its eyelashes closed

Singing

—*Translated from the Greek by Kimon Friar*

(from *The Forgotten Woman*, 1945)

The Dream

> *Notre voyage à nous est entièrement*
> *imaginaire. Voilà sa force.*
> —F.C. CÉLINE

The everliving dream
caresses its white hair

Boys undress in the light
throw the ball and shout in triumph
a Frankish priest points with his fingers at Lycabbétos
a naked boy smiles at the girls
they grow tall in their branches they shout
he is crippled he is crippled
afterwards they plunge in shame in the red water

Young women undress in the shadow
in the endless harbor frightened
a surgeon on the balcony opens and closes his lancets
tired stevedores lie in wait
to cut the ship's cables
to tear the unvirginal dresses to tatters
to mutiny and hang the captain
from the large mast of the sky
for women to clench their fingers
to close their eyes to sigh
to show their teeth their tongues

The voyage of joy begins

The suffering woman undressed in the dark
she swarmed up the wretched house and
stopped the futile music
she laughed in the mirror lifted her hands
painted her face with the color
of an expectation saw the sun
in her watch and then remembered:

"Look, the poem has come true
and the illegitimate boy and the color
make a gift of joy
and how can they photograph this place
it is a place of hypocrisy
it is a land where boys
who have lost their innocence lie in ambush
and spread out their hands to the open windows
that the sick kisses might fall
that the young short-lived orphans
might fall weeping from the windows
squeezing in their wounded hands
a tuft of white hair

From the very ancient dream"

—Translated from the Greek by Kimon Friar

(from *The Forgotten Woman*, 1945)

The Forgotten Woman

I

This furrow is not a furrow of blood
this ship is not a ship of storm
this wall is not a wall of sensuality
this crumb is not a crumb of holiday
this dog is not a dog of flowers
this tree is not a tree electrical
this house is not a house of hesitation

The white old woman is not an old woman about to die

They are a spoonful of sweet wine the vigor of joy
for the life of the forgotten woman

II
The forgotten woman opens her window
she opens her eyes
trucks with women dressed in black pass by below
who display their naked sex
who one-eyed drivers who blaspheme
by her Christ and her Virgin Mary
the women in black wish her evil
and let them throw carnations at her steeped in blood
from the effervescence of their sensual gardens
from the evaporation of gasoline in a cloud of smoke
the drivers
tear through the cloud and call her prostitute
but she a Dolorous Virgin
with her beloved amid the icons
precisely as time has preserved him
with the candles of all the betrayed
who marched to death between the daisies and the camomile
with beldames servants and mountain stars
with swords that slashed through throats and palm trees

III
The forgotten woman stretches out her white hand
takes however a piece of colored glass and sings
"I call to you not from within the dream
but from among these splinters of multi-colored glasses
yet you always recede
now indeed your face frightens me truly
no matter how much I try to match these broken glasses
I can no longer face you wholly
at times I only construct your head
among a thousand other savage heads that estrange me
at times only your beloved body
among a thousand other amputated bodies
at times only again only your blessed hand
among a thousand other outflung hands
that encumber my feet under my dresses
they blindfold me with their black handkerchiefs
they command me to walk and not turn back my head
to see your eyes shattering"

IV

The forgotten woman in the depths of her victorious sleep
holding an apple in her right hand caressing the sea with the other
suddenly unfolds her beautiful eyes
it is only a breeze the roar of a cannon
it is only the bicyclist his beloved and a bouquet of flowers
it is the clamor of the heart the smoke of minefields
it is hatred bodies that couple in rage and sink
it is a dreadful kiss on the frontiers of sensuality
where five deaths may be found sown among the poppies
it is the shadow of her lover passing by

V

Forty years later the forgotten woman shall uproot these words. And shall
I say that on this street miracles happen? No. Miracles happen only in
haunted churches. Shall I speak of the man who became a tree and of his
mouth that sprouted with flowers? I am shy but I must speak no matter if
no one believes me. The only one who could have believed me was killed
there before the altar, a few naked boys stoned him to death. They wanted
to kill a wolf-hound they wanted to sing a song they wanted to kiss a
woman. At all events they killed him and cut him in two with a saber.
From the waist up they put him in a window as a statue. From the waist
down they taught him to walk like a toddling child. He did not seem wor-
thy enough to become a good statue for his eye would not turn white. And
then again his feet cut a great many crazy capers and frightened the women
who spend the night in windows. Now from the sides of his lips two small
bitter leaves have sprouted. Extremely green. Is he a flower or a man? Is he
a man or a statue? Is he a statue or a lurking death? Forty years later the
forgotten woman shall uproot these words.

VI

The forgotten woman is the soldier who was crucified
the forgotten woman is the clock that stopped
the forgotten woman is the branch that caught fire
the forgotten woman is the needle that broke
the forgotten woman is the tomb of Christ that blossomed
the forgotten woman is the hand that aimed
the forgotten woman is the back that shuddered
the forgotten woman is the kiss that sickened
the forgotten woman is the knife that missed
the forgotten woman is the mud that dried
the forgotten woman is the fever that fell

—*Translated from the Greek by Kimon Friar*

(from *The Forgotten Woman*, 1945)

The Factory

Factory factory
of night and fire
with large suns made of roses
fire ladders
poplar trees—ghosts with red leaves
despairing birds tied with harsh
white string
frightful toys

The bride smiles
with soiled arm
with cracked hand
with painted nails
the ship anchored by the pierside
and further down the storm
and further down the drowned man

He She

The tired horses by the rain's side
thirst
and further beyond thirst

The Poet

Kept his gardens hidden in his mouth
that burned and filled the land with smoke

Factory factory
fright and flame

—Translated from the Greek by Kimon Friar

(from *Ballads*, 1948)

The Sheep

O head of mind filled with dream
hands of mine filled with mud

Well should I also sing of the rain
when Pontius Pilate walked in the streets

no one recognized his face
in the darkness in the desert next to the cables
when Jesus was multiplying the fishes
one man leant on a hedge
another on a blind bridge
another on a ruined house
when Jesus was multiplying the fishes
and the sea was casting up on land
her wild white sheep
Pontius Pilate walked in the streets
no one however recognized his joy
Pontius Pilate the first river mate
with the cage his hungry birds
the garden his lost flowers
the two embraced on the hill
the two sighed in the arcade
the two swooned under the cypress tree
when the sea once more gathered
her wild white sheep
and put them to sleep in her bitter arms

—*Translated from the Greek by Kimon Friar*

(from *With Face to the Wall*, 1952)

The Clock

Black is the sun
in my mother's
garden
with a tall green
top hat
my father
would bewitch the birds
and I
with a deaf
and distrustful clock
count the years
and
wait for my parents

—*Translated from the Greek by Kimon Friar*

(from *The Stroll*, 1960)

Ectoplasms

In my grave
I walk in agitation
up and down
up and down

I hear things around me howling
ideas-automobiles
autombiles-ideas

Men pass by
they speak, they laugh
for me

they tell truths
they tell lies
for me, for me!

—Don't, I shout to them
don't speak
about my dead loves

they will waken
they will gouge out your eyes!

—Translated from the Greek by Kimon Friar

(from *Color Wounds*, 1980)

PERMISSIONS

"The Difficult Sunday," "Beauty," "The Dream," "The Forgotten Woman," "The Factory, "The Sheep," "The Clock" and "Ectoplasms"
Reprinted from *Selected Poems*, trans. by Kimon Friar (Old Chatham, New York: Sachem Press, 1982). Copyright ©1982 by Kimon Friar. Reprinted by permission of Sachem Press.

Saint-John Perse [Alexis Saint-Léger Léger] [b. Guadeloupe/France] 1887–1975

Born in Saint-Léger-les-Feuilles, Guadeloupe, Saint-John Perse spent his adolescence in France and his training at the University of Bordeaux, where he received his degree in law in 1910. His earliest poems are from that period.

Saint-John Perse

In 1916, he entered the Foreign Service, and was sent to China, remaining there until 1921. Upon his return to France, he continued to rise in rank in the Service, eventually serving as Secretary General for Foreign Affairs. Throughout this period, he continued to write, without publishing. With the rise of the Nazi-run Vichy government, Saint-John Perse was dismissed from service, and several of his poetic manuscripts were confiscated by the German government. In Washington, D.C., where he took up residence, he continued writing. In 1960 he received the Nobel Prize for literature, and seven years later he returned to France.

His earliest poems, *Éloges*, were published in 1911 and revised in 1925. These works celebrate his childhood in the Antilles and events in West Indies history. The earliest of these poems, "Images à Crusoé," was written when he was just seventeen years of age. *Anabase* (1924, *Anabasis*, 1930) contain some of the few poems written during his diplomatic service period. These works contain the hallmark qualities of Saint-John Perse's writing: radical elipsis, an almost biblical quality of language, and compressed use of language underlying a highly rhapsodic narrative.

His other major works include *Exil* (1942), *Poème à l'étrangére* (1943), *Pluies* (1944), *Neiges* (1945), *Vents* (1946), and *Amers* (1957).

BOOKS OF POETRY:

Éloges (Paris, 1911; revised, 1925); *Anabase* (Paris, 1924; revised, 1948); *Exil* (with "Pluies" and "Neiges") in *Quatre poèmes, 1941-1944* (Buenos Aires, 1944); *Vents* (Paris, 1946); *Amers* (Paris, 1957); *Chronique* (Marseilles, 1959; Paris, 1960); *Oiseaux* (Paris, 1962, 1963): *Sécheresse* (Paris, 1974); *Nocturne* (Paris, 1972).

ENGLISH LANGUAGE TRANSLATIONS:

Anabasis, trans. by T. S. Eliot (New York: Harcourt, Brace and Company, 1938); *Éloges and Other Poems*, trans. by Louise Varèse (New York: W. W. Norton & Company, 1944); *Selected Poems*, edited by Mary Ann Caws (New York: New Directions, 1982).

Pictures for Crusoe

The Bells

Old man with naked hands,
   cast up among men again, Crusoe!
   you wept, I imagine, when from the Abbey towers, like a tide, the sob of the bells
poured over the City...
   O Despoiled!
   You wept to remember the surf in the moonlight; the whistlings of the more distant
shores; the strange music that is born and is muffled under the folded wing of the
night,
   like the linked circles that are the waves of a conch, or the amplications of the clam-
ors under the sea....

The Goatskin Parasol

It is there in the gray odor of dust under the eaves of the attic. It is beneath the three-
legged table; it is between the box of sand for the cat and the unhooped barrel piled
with feathers.

The Bow

Before the hissings of the hearth, numb beneath your flowered wrapper, you watch
the soft undulating fins of the flames.—But a snapping fissures the singing darkness:
it is your bow, on its nail, that has burst. And it splits along the whole length of its
secret fiber, like the dead pod in the hands of the warrior tree.

The Seed

You buried it in a flowerpot, the purple seed that had stuck to your goatskin jacket.
   It has not sprouted.

The Book

And then what a wail in the mouth of the hearth, a night of long rains on their march
toward the city, stirred in your heart the obscure birth of speech:
   "...Of a luminous exile—and more distant already than the storm that is rolling—
how can I, O Lord, keep the ways that you opened?

"...Will you leave me only this confusion of evening—having, for so long a day, nour-
ished me on the salt of your solitude,

"witness of your silences, of your shadow, and of the great blasts of your voice?"

—Thus you lamented in the confusion of evening.

But sitting by the window opposite the stretch of wall across the way, having failed
to resuscitate the lost splendor,

you would open the Book,

and letting your worn finger wander among the prophecies, your gaze far away, you
awaited the moment of departure, the rising of the great wind that would suddenly
tear you away, like the typhoon, parting the clouds before your waiting eyes.

—Translated from the French by Louise Varèse

(from *Éloges*, 1911, 1925)

from *Anabasis*

II

In busy lands are the greatest silences, in busy lands with the locusts at noon.

I tread, you tread in a land of high slopes clothed in balm, where the linen of the
Great is exposed to dry.

We step over the gown of the Queen, all of lace with two brown stripes (and how
well the acid body of a woman can stain a gown at the armpit).

We step over the gown of the Queen's daughter, all of lace with two bright stripes
(and how well the lizard's tongue can catch ants at the armpit).

And perhaps the day does not pass but the same man may burn with desire for a
woman and for her daughter.

Knowing laugh of the dead, let this fruit be peeled for us...How, under the wild rose
is there no more grace to the world?

Comes from this side of the world a great purple doom on the waters. Rises the
wind, the sea-wind. And the linen exposed to dry

scatters! like a priest torn in pieces...

IV

Such is the way of the world and I have nothing but good to say of it.—Foundation of
the City. Stone and bronze. Thorn fires at dawn

bared these great

green stones, and viscid like the bases of temples, of latrines,

and the mariner at sea whom our smoke reached saw that the earth to the summit
had changed its form (great tracts of burnt-over land seen afar and these operations
of channeling the living waters on the mountains).

Thus was the City founded and placed in the morning under the labials of a holy name. The encampments are razed from the hills! And we who are there in the wooden galleries,
head bare and foot bare in the freshness of the world,
what have we to laugh at, but what have we to laugh at, as we sit, for a disembarka-tion of girls and mules?
and what is there to say, since the dawn, of all this people under sail?—Arrivals of grain! ...And the ships taller than Ilion under the white peacock of heaven, having crossed the bar, hove to
in this deadwater where floats a dead ass. (We must ordain the fate of this pale meaningless river, color of grass-hoppers crushed in their sap.)

In the great fresh noise of the yonder bank, the blacksmiths are masters of their fires! The cracking of whips in the new streets unloads whole wainsful of unhatched evils. O mules, our shadows under the copper sword! four restive heads knotted to the fist make a living cluster against the blue. The founders of asylums meet beneath a tree and find their ideas for the choice of situations. They teach me the meaning and the purpose of the buildings: front adorned, back blind; the galleries of laterite, the vesti-bules of black stone and the pools of clear shadow for libraries; cool places for wares of the druggist. And then come the bankers blowing into their keyes. And already in the streets a man sang alone, one of those who paint on their brow the cipher of their god. (Perpetual crackling of insects in this quarter of vacant lots and rubbish.) ...And this is no time to tell you, no time to reckon our alliances with the people of the other shore; water presented in skins, commandeering of cavalry for the dockworks and princes paid in currency of fish. (A child sorrowful as the death of apes—one that had an elder sister of great beauty—offered us a quail in a slipper of rose-colored satin.)

...Solitude! the blue egg laid by a great sea-bird, and the bays at morning all littered with gold lemons!—Yesterday it was! The bird made off!
Tomorrow the festivals and tumults, the avenues planted with podded trees, and the dustmen at dawn bearing away huge pieces of dead palmtrees, fragments of giant wings... Tomorrow the festivals,
the election of harbor-masters, the voices practicing in the suburbs and, under the moist incubation of storms,
the yellow town, casque'd in shade, with the girls' drawers hanging at the windows.

*

...At the third lunation, those who kept watch on the hilltops folded their canvas. The body of a woman was burnt in the sands. And a man strode forth at the threshold of the desert—profession of his father: dealer in scent-bottles.

X

Select a wide hat with the brim seduced. The eye withdraws by a century into the provinces of the soul. Through the gate of living chalk we see the things of the plain: living things,
excellent things!

sacrifice of colts on the tombs of children, purification of widows among the roses and consignments of green birds in the courtyards to do honor to the old men;
many things on the earth to hear and to see, living things among us!
celebrations of open air festivals for the name-day of great trees and public rites in honor of a pool; consecration of black stones perfectly round, water-dowsing in dead places, dedication of cloths held up on poles, as the gates of the passes, and loud acclamations under the walls for the mutilation of adults in the sun, for the publication of the bride-sheets!
many other things too at the level of our eyes: dressing the sores of animals in the suburbs, stirring of the crowds before sheep-shearers, well-sinkers and horse-gelders; speculations in the breath of harvests and turning of hay on the roofs, on the prongs of forks; building of enclosures of rose red terra cotta, of terraces for meat-drying, of galleries for priests, of quarters for captains; the vast court of the horse-doctor; the fatigue parties for upkeep of muleways, of zig-zag roads through the gorges; foundation of hospices in vacant places; the invoicing at arrival of caravans, and disbanding of escorts in the quarter of money-changers; budding popularities under the penthouse, in front of the frying vats; protestation of bills of credit; destruction of albino animals, of white worms in the soil; fires of bramble and thorn in places defiled by death, the making of a fine bread of barley and sesame; or else of spelt; and the firesmoke of mankind everywhere...

ha! all conditions of men in their ways and manners; eaters of insects, of water fruits; those who bear poultices, those who bear riches; the husbandman, and the young noble horsed; the healer with needles, and the salter; the toll-gatherer, the smith; vendors of sugar, of cinnamon, of white metal drinking cups and of lanthorns; he who fashions a leather tunic, wooden shoes and olive-shaped buttons; he who dresses a field; and the man of no trade: the man with the falcon, the man with the flute, the man with bees; he who has his delight in the pitch of his voice, he who makes it his business to contemplate a green stone; he who burns for his pleasure a thornfire on his roof; he who makes on the ground his bed of sweet-smelling leaves, lies down there and rests; he who thinks out designs of green pottery for fountains; and he who has traveled far and dreams of departing again; he who has dwelt in the country of great rains; the dicer, the knucklebone player, the juggler; or he who has spread on the ground his reckoning tablets; he who has his opinions on the use of a gourd; he who drags a dead eagle like a faggot on his tracks (and the plumage is given, not sold, for fletching); he who gathers pollen in a wooden jar (and my delight, says he, is in this yellow color);

he who eats fritters, the maggots of the palmtree, or raspberries; he who fancies the flavor of tarragon; he who dreams of green pepper, or else he who chews fossil gum, who lifts a conch to his ear, or he who sniffs the odor of genius in the freshly cracked stone; he who thinks of the flesh of women, the lustful; he who sees his soul reflected in a blade; the man learned in sciences, in onomastic; the man well thought of in councils, he who names fountains, he who makes a public gift of seats in the shady places, of dyed wool for the wise men; and has great bronze jars, for thirst, planted at the crossways; better still, he who does nothing, such a one and such in his manners, and so many others still! those who collect quails in the wrinkled land, those who hunt among the furze for green-speckled eggs, those who dismount to pick things up, agates, a pale blue stone which they cut and fashion at the gates of the suburbs (into cases, tobacco-boxes, brooches, or into balls to be rolled between the hands of the paralyzed); those who whistling paint boxes in the open air, the man with the ivory staff, the man with the rattan chair, the hermit with hands like a girl's and the disbanded warrior who has planted his spear at the threshold to tie up a monkey...ha! all sorts of men in their ways and fashions, and of a sudden! behold in his evening robes and summarily settling in turn all questions of precedence, the Story-Teller who stations himself at the foot of the turpentine tree...

O genealogist upon the market-place! how many chronicles of familes and connections? —and may the dead seize the quick, as is said in the tables of the law, if I have not seen each thing in its own shadow and the virtue of its age: the stores of books and annals, the astronomer's storehouses and the beauty of a place of sepulture, of very old temples under the palmtrees, frequented by a mule and three white hens—and beyond my eye's circuit, many a secret doing on the routes: striking of camps upon tidings which I know not, effronteries of the hill tribes, and passage of rivers on skinjars; horsemen bearing letters of alliance, the ambush in the vineyard, forays of robbers in the depths of gorges and manoeuvres over field to ravish a woman, bargaindriving and plots, coupling of beasts in the forests before the eyes of children, convalescence of prophets in byres, the silent talk of two men under a tree...

but over and above the actions of men on the earth, many omens on the way, many seeds on the way, and under unleavened fine weather, in one great breath of the earth, the whole feather of harvest!...

until the hour of evening when the female star, pure and pledged in the sky heights...

Plough-land of dream! Who talks of building?—I have seen the earth parceled out in vast spaces and my thought is not heedless of the navigator.

—Translated from the French by T. S. Eliot

(from *Anabase*, 1924)

Nocturne

Now! they are ripe, these fruits of a jealous fate. From our dream grown, on our blood fed, and haunting the purple of our nights, they are the fruits of long concern, they are the fruits of long desire, they were our most secret accomplices and, often verging upon avowal, drew us to their ends out of the abyss of our nights.... Praise to the first dawn, now they are ripe and beneath the purple, these fruits of an imperious fate.— We do not find our liking here.

Sun of being, betrayal! Where was the fraud, where was the offense? where was the fault and where the flaw, and the error, which is the error? Shall we trace the theme back to its birth? shall we relive the fever and the torment? ...Majesty of the rose, we are not among your adepts: our blood goes to what is bitterer, our care to what is more severe, our roads are uncertain, and deep is the night out of which our gods are torn. Dog roses and black briars populate for us the shore of shipwreck.

Now they are ripening, these fruits of another shore: "Sun of being, shield me!"— turncoat's words. And those who have seen him pass will say: who was that man, and which his home? Did he go alone at dawn to show the purple of his nights? ...Sun of being, Prince and Master! our works are scattered, our tasks without honor and our grain without harvest: the binder of sheaves awaits, at the evening's ebb.—Behold, they are dyed with our blood, these fruits of a stormy fate.

At the gait of a binder of sheaves life goes, without hatred or ransom.

—Translated from the French by Richard Howard

(from *Nocturne*, 1972)

Edith Södergran [Finland/writing in Swedish] 1892–1923

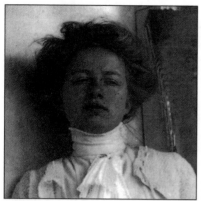

Self-portrait by Edith Södergran

Born of Finland-Swedish parents, Edith Södergran was educated at a German school in St. Petersburg. She contracted tuberculosis early in her life and was a patient in the sanatorium at Davos, Switzerland in 1912–13 and again in 1913–14. Accordingly, her early work is reminiscent of the German romantics, particularly of Heine, rather than being influenced by her native language.

In the beginning of World War I, she settled with her mother at Raivola on the Karelian Isthmus of Finland, an area in which most of the natives spoke Finnish. Extremely isolated, Södergran expanded her girlhood fantasies of taking the Finnish literary world by storm, and made two trips to Helsinki to show her manuscripts. There she met Hugo Bergroth, who persuaded her to abandon the German language for Swedish. Yet Södergran was little influenced by contemporary Swedish writing, but rather looked back to C. J. L. Almqvist of the late 18th and early 19th century, whose romantic heroine in *Drottningens juvelsmycke* was androgynous.

It is presumed that an unsuccessful love affair was the inspiration of her first book, *Dikter*, of 1916. The reaction to this book was one of open ridicule or perplexity at best. A final attempt to enter the Finland-Swedish literary circles ended in disaster, and Södergran fled back to Raivola. The October revolution took away the family savings in Russia, and they were left with poverty and illness. A period of severe depression followed, and it was only after reading Nietzsche and after the major events of the Finnish civil war that Södergran was awakened to a new sense of possibility, expressed in *Septemberlyran* (The September Lyre) of 1918. That book, however, only brought severe doubts about her sanity. One positive review by the critic and novelist Hagar Olsson led to a close and sustained friendship between the two women and to the composition of *Rosenaltaret* (The Rose Altar) of 1919, which advocated a cult of female beauty and an erotic "sisterhood."

Her conversion, brought about by the writings of Rudolf Steiner and a vision of primitive Christian ritual, led Södergran to abandon poetry after 1920 until the very end of her life. By the 1930s Södergran's work had become broadly admired, and her home in Raivola became a shrine to aspiring lyricists. Among her many admirers were the Swedish poet Gunnar Ekelöf (see *PIP Anthology, Vol. 1*) and the Finnish poet Uuno Kailas (1901–1933).

BOOKS OF POETRY:

Dikter (Helsinki: Holger Schildts Förlagsaktiebolag, 1916); *Septemberlyran* (Helsinki: Holger Schildts Förlagsaktiebolag, 1918); *Rosenaltaret* (Helsinki: Holger Schildts Förlagsaktiebolag, 1919); *Framtidens skugga* (Helsinki: Holger Schildts Förlagsaktiebolag); *Landet som icke är* (Helsinki: Holger Schildts Förlagsaktiebolag, 1925); *Samlade dikter*, edited by Gunnar Tideström (Helsinki:

Holger Schildts Förlagsaktiebolag, 1949 and later editions); *Samlade skrifter I: Dikter och aforismer*, edited by Holger Lillqvist (Helsinki: Holger Schildts Förlagsaktiebolag, 1990).

ENGLISH LANGUAGE TRANSLATIONS:

Poems, trans. by Gounil Brown (Croesor, Wales: Zena Publications, 1990); *Love & Solitude: Selected Poems 1916-1923*, trans. by Stina Katchadourian (Seattle: Fjord Press, 1992).

Violet Twilights

Violet twilights I carry within me from my ancient past,
naked virgins playing with galloping centaurs...
Yellow sunshine days with bright glances,
only sunbeams pay proper homage to a tender female body...
No man has yet arrived, has ever been, will ever be...
A man is a false mirror that the sun's daughter hurls against the cliffs in rage,
a man is a lie, incomprehensible to pure children,
a man is a rotten fruit rejected by proud lips.

Beautiful sisters, come high up to the strongest rocks,
we are all fighting women, heroines, horsewomen,
eyes of innocence, brows of heaven, rosy faces,
heavy breakers and soaring birds,
we are the least expected and the darkest red,
tigerspots, taut strings, fearless stars.

—*Translated from the Finland-Swedish by Stina Katchadourian*

(from *Dikter,* 1916)

Vierge Moderne

I am no woman. I am a neuter.
I am a child, a page-boy, and a bold decision,
I am a laughing streak of a scarlet sun...
I am a net for all voracious fish,
I am a toast to every woman's honor,
I am a step toward luck and toward ruin,
I am a leap in freedom and the self...
I am the whisper of desire in a man's ear,
I am the soul's shivering, the flesh's longing and denial,
I am an entry sign to new paradises.
I am a flame, searching and brave,
I am water, deep yet bold only to the knees,
I am fire and water, honestly combined, on free terms...

—Translated from the Finland-Swedish by Stina Katchadourian

(from *Dikter*, 1916)

Hell

Oh the magnificence of hell!
In hell no one speaks of death.
Hell is walled up in the bowels of the earth
and adorned with glowing flowers...
In hell no one says an empty word...
In hell no one has drunk and no one has slept
and no one rests and no one sits still.
In hell no one speaks but everyone screams,
there, tears are not tears and all grief is powerless.
In hell no one falls ill and no one tires.
Hell is constant and eternal.

—Translated from the Finland-Swedish by Stina Katchadourian

(from *Dikter*, 1916)

Marches of the Future

Tear down all triumphal arches—
the arches are too low.
Make room for our fantastic marches!
The future is heavy—build the bridges
for eternity.
Giants, carry rocks from the ends of the world!
Demons, pour oil under the cauldrons!
Monster, gauge the measures with your tail!
Rise up in the heavens, heroic figures,
fateful hands—begin your work.
Break loose a piece from heaven. Blazing.
We shall grapple and fight.
We shall struggle for the future's manna.
Rise up, heralds,
even now strangely visible from afar,
the day demands your drumbeat.

—*Translated from the Finland-Swedish by Stina Katchadourian*

(from *Septemberlyran*, 1918)

PERMISSIONS

"Violet Twilights," "Vierge Moderne," "Hell," and "Marches of the Future"
Reprinted from *Love & Solitude: Selected Poems 1916–1923*, trans. by Stina Katchadourian (Seattle: Fjord Press, 1992). Copyright ©1981, 1985, 1992 by Stina Katchadourian. Reprinted by permission of Fjord Press.

Alfonsina Storni [Argentina]
1892–1938

Born of Italian parents in Switzerland, Alfonsina Storni's parents had emigrated to Argentina in 1885. They returned to Switzerland again in 1889 for an extended visit, where Alfonsina was born. She was three at their return to San Juan.

Almost immediately the family had great financial difficulty. Her father took to drinking, neglecting his business, and was absent much of the time. Storni's mother, Paula, struggled to keep the family fed and in clothing, moving to Rosario after the father's death in 1906. At thirteen, accordingly, Alfonsina began to work at a nearby hat factory to supplement her family's income. During this period, however, she was recognized by a local theatrical company and began touring with them.

In 1909 Storni enrolled in a school for rural teachers. She also secretly participated in the chorus of a theater, and when her theatrical activities were discovered, the incident created a minor scandal. Storni ran away, leaving a suicide note.

In 1912 she arrived in Buenos Aires with her diploma and an infant son, eventually finding employment working as a cashier. Later she worked at an import firm. Her first poems began to appear during this period, and in 1916 her first book, *La inquietud del rosal* (The Restlessness of the Rosebush) was published. The poems revealed her affinities to European modernism and symbolic writing. But later she denounced this work and attempted to prevent it from inclusion in collections.

Her book, however, in its complaints against sexual injustice, became a sensation in Buenos Aires, and she soon became involved in the literary world of the city, one of the first women to participate in that all-male society. Her dramatic readings at the poetic events led her friends to help her get a position, created especially for her, at the Lavarden Children's Theater and a chair in reading at the Normal School of Modern Languages. She devoted her energies for the next several years to teaching. She also published several volumes of poetry, *El dulce dano* (1918, The Secret Pain), *Irremediablemente* (1919, Irremediably), and *Languidez* (1920, Languor).

Throughout the 1920s she directed the Teatro Infantil, a position which the city had created for her. But her financial security and professional admiration did not assuage her sense of gender injustice or her own dismay at having to be dependent upon men. Her work *Ocre* in 1925 began a change in her writing from a heightened romantic sensibility to concern with the status of women throughout the century. Later works include *El mundo de siete pozos* (1934, The World of Seven Wells) and *Mascarilla y trebol* (1938, Mask and Clover), the latter appearing after her death.

In bad health and suffering from depression, Storni walked into the sea in October 1938 to her death.

BOOKS OF POETRY:

La inquietud del rosal (1916); *Irremediablement* (1919); *Languidez* (1920); *Ocre* (1925); *Mundo de siete pozos* (1934); *Antologia Poetica* (1936); *Mascarilla y trebol* (1938); *Obra poética* (1946, 1952); *Obras completas* (1964).

ENGLISH LANGUAGE TRANSLATIONS:

Selected Poems, trans. by Marion Freeman, Mary Crow, Jim Normington, and Kay Short (Fredonia, New York: White Wine Press, 1987).

You Want Me White

You'd like me to be white as dawn,
You'd like me to be made of foam,
You wish I were mother of pearl,
A lily
Chaste above all others.
Of delicate perfume.
A closed bud.

Not one ray of the moon
Should have filtered me,
Not one daisy
Should have called me sister.
You want me to be snowy,
You want me to be white,
You want me to be like dawn.

You who have held all the wineglasses
In your hand,
Your lips stained purple
With fruit and honey
You who in the banquet
Crowned with young vines
Made toasts with your flesh to Bacchus.
You who in the gardens
Black with Deceit
Dressed in red
Ran to your Ruin.

You who keep your skeleton
Well preserved, intact,
I don't know yet
Through what miracles
You want to make me white
(God forgive you),
You want to make me chaste
(God forgive you),
You want to make me like dawn!

Run away to the woods;
Go to the mountain;
Wash your mouth;
Get to know the wet earth
With your hands;
Feed your body
With bitter roots;
Drink from the rocks;
Sleep on the white frost;
Renew your tissue
With the salt of rocks and water;
Talk to the birds
And get up at dawn.
And when your flesh
Has returned to you,
and when you have put
Your soul back into it,
Your soul which was left entangled
In all the bedrooms,
Then, my good man,
Ask me to be white,
Ask me to be snowy,
Ask me to be chaste.

—Translated from the Spanish by Marion Freeman and Mary Crow

(from *El dulce dano*, 1918)

The Moment

A city of gray bones
lies abandoned at my feet.

The piles of bones
are separated by black trenches,
the streets,
divided by them,
ordered, raised by them.
In the city, bristling with two million men,
I haven't a single one to love me.

The sky, even grayer
than the city,
descends over me,
takes over my life,
stops up my arteries,
turns off my voice...

However,
the world,
like a whirlwind
from which I can't escape,
turns round a dead point:
my heart.

—*Translated by Marion Freeman and Mary Crow*

(from *Mundo de siete pozos*, 1934)

And the Head Began to Burn

On the black
wall
a square
opened up
that looked out
over the void.

And the moon rolled
up to the window;
it stopped
and said to me:
"I'm not moving from here;
I'm looking at you.

I don't want to grow
or get thin.
I'm the infinite
flower
that opens up
in the square hole
in your house.

I no longer want
to roll on
behind
the lands
that you don't know,
my butterfly,
sipper of shadows.

Or raise phantoms
over the far off
cupolas
that drink me.

I'm watching
I see you."

And I didn't answer.
A head was sleeping
under my hands.

White,
like you,
moon.

The wells of its eyes
held a dark
water
streaked
with luminous snakes.

And suddenly
my head
began to burn
like the stars
at twilight.

And my hands
were stained
with a phosphorescent
substance.

And with it
I burn
the houses
of men,
the forests
of beasts.

—Translated from the Spanish by Marion Freeman

(from *Mundo de siete pozos*, 1934)

Departure

A road
to the limit:
high golden doors
close it off;
deep galleries;
arcades...

The air has no weight;
the doors stand by themselves
in the emptiness;
they disintegrate into golden dust;
they close, they open;
they go down to the algae
tombs;
they come up loaded with coral.

Patrols,
there are patrols of columns;
the doors hide
behind the blue parapets;
water bursts into fields of forget-me-nots;
it tosses up deserts of purple crystals;
it incubates great emerald worms;
it plaits its innumerable arms.

A rain of wings,
now;
pink angels
dive like arrows
into the sea.
I could walk on them
without sinking.
A path of ciphers
for my feet;
columns of numbers
for each step—
submarine.

They carry me:
invisible vines
stretch out their hooks
from the horizon.
My neck creaks.
I walk.
The water holds its own.
My shoulders open into wings.
I touch the ends of the sky
with their tips.
I wound it.
The sky's blood
bathing the sea...
poppies, poppies,
there is nothing but poppies.

I grow light:
the flesh falls from my bones.
Now.
The sea rises through the channels
of my spine.

Now.
The sky rolls through the bed
of my veins.
Now.
The sun! the sun!
Its last rays
envelop me,
push me:
I am a spindle
I spin, spin, spin, spin!

—Translated from the Spanish by Marion Freeman

(from *Antologia Poetica*, 1936)

Supertelephone

"Can I speak to Horatio?" I know that now
you have a nest of doves in your bladder,
and your crystal motorcycle flies
silently through the air.

"Papa?" I dreamed that your flask
swelled up like the Tupungato river;
it still holds your anger and my poems.
Pour me a drop. Thanks. Now I feel fine.

I'll be seeing you both very soon. Come to meet me
with that frog I killed at our country house
in San Juan; poor frog—we stoned it to death.

It looked at us like an ox, and my two cousins
finished it off; later it had a funeral
with skillets banging, and roses followed it.

—Translated from the Spanish by Marion Freeman

(from *Mascarilla y trebol*, 1938)

Suggestion of Bird Song

Death hasn't been born yet, it's asleep
on a rose-colored beach. Consider the Greek:
he didn't die from infamy and hemlock;
and above the Acropolis he burns.

Who told you that envy's finger
streaked my clothes with yellow?
It was a butterfly overloaded
with pollen passing by.

Do you hear? Rats in the offices
aren't biting the boss's soles;
That's a fine rain of dry

violets that rustles as it falls;
and the young man's unraveling heart
is William's heroic apple.

—Translated from the Spanish by Marion F. Freeman

Sea Winds

My heart was a flower
of foam;
one petal of snow,
another of salt;
the sea wind took it
and put it
into a rough hand

hardened by the sea.
So fine a lace
on a rough hand.
How to drop anchor?
A gust of wind
picked it up again;
carried it tumbling
through immensity.
It's still drifting.
It tangles in the chains
that strike the flanks
of ships...oh!

—Translated from the Spanish by Mary Crow

Circles with No Center

Sky sponge,
green flesh of the sea,
I had to travel
along your smooth tracks.

Ahead, roads
not for walking parted;
alongside, highways
for navigating opened;
and behind, routes for
retracing the way
led off.

Long nights and days
a prow cut you ceaselessly
but your center never changed,
green circle of the sea.

My flesh didn't want to burn
on your cold emerald.
My heart turned green
as the flesh of the sea.

I said to my body: Be reborn!
To my heart: Don't stop!
My body longed to put down roots,
green roots into the sea's flesh.

The boat that carried me
knew only how to weigh anchor,
but the body containing me
remained ecstatic on the sea.

Circles circled above
and circles rose from the depth of the sea;
fishes lifted their heads
and started to yell.

—Translated from the Spanish by Mary Crow

Jorge Guillén [Spain]
1893–1984

A new translation of Guillén's poetry, *Horses in the Air and Other Poems*, trans. by Cola Franzen (San Francisco: City Lights Books, 1999) was announced as *The PIP Anthology of World Poetry of the 20th Century*, volume 1 was going to press. Because of the excellence of this new translation, and the small number of poems presented in volume 1, we have included five poems from the new book here.

The Exile

> *Corroborating forever the triumph of things.*
> —WALT WHITMAN

The atmosphere, the very atmosphere unravels.
Invisible in its graceless fiber
the object disavows even itself.
The gentle air prowls bent by squalls.
Everything is nebulous. The moon cannot be missing.
This way, so hidden,
is it you, moon, erasing and blurring everything?
Clumsy, drunk perhaps,
remembering so little of our lives

The world fits into our forgetting.

This dark tangible dankness smells of bridge
with well-worn stone railing
for mock musing about suicide.

Zero is always there, central. In this plaza
so many streets are cancelled out and undone

And suddenly
        Out of the way!
                Smooth ruthless

discreet
a treacherous bicycle whizzes past.
Treacherous momentum of pure profile
rushing toward
what subtle
goal
without making a sound?
The impending moment throbs.
The world fits into our forgetting?

Between two breaths
from below, a cloud now splits
showing a hint of ravaged sky.
The bicycle
slips past and plummets into a chaos
modest still.

"What is this?
Chaos, perhaps?"
                "Oh,
the fog, nothing more, the silly fog.
The *No*
with no demon, the dallying darkness
that never destroyed anything.
It's late now to dream up *Nothing*."

Give me back, darkness, give me back what's mine:
the blessed things, their bulk and their dew.

—Translated from the Spanish by Cola Franzen

(from *Cántico*, 1928)

Invasion

I want to sleep and lean over
without moving toward darkness.
But the mind is a path
that pierces every wall.

The infant sun is rising.
I hear the trot of a horse.

Spans of a bridge open.
Not wanting to seek I find.

The horse has left me
going its way, so alien.
I don't listen. The noise unleashed
by the light grazes me.

Sleep, rest, toil.
Horse, car, bell.
Living is not dreaming. What if
I invent my window.

Now the horse is thought.
It trots inside me and trots outside.
The window gives a breath
of a real invasion.

—*Translated from the Spanish by Cola Franzen*

(from *Clamor, tiempo de histoira*, 1960)

MARGINAL NOTES: WHITMAN

Leaves of Grass in the Wind

> *I strike up for a new world.*
> —"Proto-Leaf."

There are many wise prophets
who disturb us with prophecies.
The spirited trumpets sound.
Would they know about future days?

Vast 21st century:
Would folly be the omen?
On Neptune's knees,
pandemonium, the planet throbs.

Unforeseen future
composed of infinite threads.
Must one climb to the peak?

Must one defend the caves?

Leaves of grass light our way,
light of inexhaustible hope.
Countering the mortal sorrow
our hearts are poised to pounce.

—Translated from the Spanish by Cola Franzen

(from *Al margen*, 1974)

MARGINAL NOTES: THE THOUSAND AND ONE NIGHTS

Expectancy

...Then I said: "Open Sesame." The door,
solemnly, secretly, smoothly, opened.
Surprised, but finding no obstacle,
I went in.

Someone within my heart was my
safeguard. Suddenly I saw a room.
Chrystal chandeliers were gleaming
over festivities still without guests.

Among mirrors, tapestries, and paintings
I was alone. Empty splendor
in reserve for a destined one.

I race toward the light and its silence,
promises of a glory now ripe
beneath my unwavering resolve. And then...

—Translated from the Spanish by Cola Franzen

(from *Al margen*, 1974)

Jackson Mac Low [U S A]
1924

After *The* PIP *Anthology of World Poetry of the 20th Century,* volume 1 went to press, Jackson Mac Low's collection *20 Forties: 20 Poems from the series "154 Forties" written and revised 1990–1999* (Gran Carnaria: Zasterle Press, 1999) was published. That book was not listed in the first volume.

In volume 1, the poem titled "Selections from 'The 11th of July'" (p. 118) was mistakenly subtitled "(19 Cub Lot Poems New York, 11 July 1946)." It should have read: "(19 Cubist Poems New York, 11 July 1946)."

Also, the photograph of Jackson Mac Low should have credited the photographer: Anne Tardos.

INDEX OF VOLUMES 1 AND 2

GREEN INTEGER
Pataphysics and Pedantry

Edited by Per Bregne
Douglas Messerli, *Publisher*

Essays, Manifestos, Statements, Speeches, Maxims,
Epistles, Diaristic Notes, Narratives, Natural Histories,
Poems, Plays, Performances, Ramblings, Revelations
and all such ephemera as may appear necessary
to bring society into a slight tremolo of confusion
and fright at least.

*

Selected Green Integer Books

History, or Messages from History Gertrude Stein [1997]
Notes on the Cinematographer Robert Bresson [1997]
The Critic As Artist Oscar Wilde [1997]
Tent Posts Henri Michaux [1997]
Eureka Edgar Allan Poe [1997]
An Interview Jean Renoir [1998]
Travels Hans Christian Andersen [1999]
On Ibsen James Joyce [1999]
A Wanderer Plays on Muted Strings Knut Hamsun [2001]
Laughter: An Essay on the Meaning of the Comic Henri Bergson [1999]
Operratics Michel Leiris [2001]
Seven Visions Sergei Paradjanov [1998]
Ghost Image Hervé Guibert [1998]
Ballets Without Music, Without Dancers, Without Anything
Louis-Ferdinand Céline [1999]
Manifestos Manifest Vicente Huidobro [2000]
Aurelia Gérard de Nerval [2001]
On Overgrown Paths Knut Hamsun [1999]
Displeasures of the Table Martha Ronk [2001]
What Is Man? Mark Twain [2000]
Poems Sappho [1999]
Suicide Circus: Selected Poems Alexei Kruchenykh [2001]
Hell Has No Limits José Donoso [1999]
To Do: Alphabets and Birthdays Gertrude Stein [2001]
Letters from Hanusse Joshua Haigh [2000]
[edited by Douglas Messerli]
Suites Federico García Lorca [2001]
Pedra Canga Tereza Albues [2001]

Green Integer EL-E-PHANT books:

The PIP Anthology of World Poetry of the 20th Century, Volume 1
Douglas Messerli, editor [2000]
The PIP Anthology of World Poetry of the 20th Century, Volume 2
Douglas Messerli, editor [2001]